T0148458

The WAY of the EARTH

RICHARD E. KUYKENDALL

Order this book online at www.trafford.com
or email orders@trafford.com

Most Trafford titles are also available at major online book retailers.

Print information available on the last page.

ISBN: 978-1-4907-9248-4 (sc)
ISBN: 978-1-4907-9260-6 (e)

Trafford rev. 12/17/2018

 www.trafford.com

North America & international
toll-free: 1 888 232 4444 (USA & Canada)
fax: 812 355 4082

Contents

Dedicated to our children

Acknowledgements

I once wrote that no book is really the work of one individual for no books are written in complete isolation. This statement is especially true with reference to this book for its entire structure is based on the gospel accounts of the life of Jesus and the book of Revelation—although its message is very different indeed from both of them!

I would like to acknowledge my infinite debt to Matthew Fox for teaching me the truth of Creation Spirituality and for providing me with an excellent doctoral program where I was able to study with Native American and Wiccan teachers such as Jose Hobday and Starhawk as well as other notables such as: Clarissa Pinkola Estes, Andrew Harvey, dream-worker, Jeremy Taylor and Oshun Priestess, Luisah Teish.

Beyond this I would like to acknowledge my debt to Carole Clark whose work enabled me to meet Drahcira. I am also thankful for Lucille Cornwell, Martha Pierce and Tom and Irma Hopkins who supported me through a period of intense change on my spiritual path.

I am grateful for my various "Spiritwind" groups which have provided me with groups of spiritually adventurous people willing to consider the teachings of Drahcira.

And finally, I am thankful for my wife, Ava who has been patient, loving and supportive beyond imagining with one who very imperfectly is attempting to live out the teachings recorded herein.

Foreword

"Imagine there's no heaven—it's easy if you try,
No hell below us—above us, only sky."
John Lennon

As long as I can remember I have been bothered by the fact that all of the founders of the world's religions have been men. Surely there must have been a woman who was spiritual enough to have begun something. And more than this, to this day many Christian denominations still will not ordain women—not to mention that most of the religions of the world will not allow a woman to serve in a leadership position. Besides this, at least in the monotheistic religions, God is a man—"Our Heavenly Father."

In Wiccan circles however there is a strong belief in the Goddess in her many guises—a belief which they feel goes back to the Great Mother of Neolithic times.

To me it was a breath of fresh air to see a woman (though admittedly fictional) in this book who was a great leader, who taught and was willing to die for what she believed in. This woman was Drahcira, Prophetess of the Earth.

Drahcira teaches the "Gospel of the Way of the Earth" in contrast to Jesus' teaching the "Gospel of the Kingdom of Heaven." Her emphasis is on the world "As It Is" now rather than in some "hereafter."

Yes, Drahcira teaches a radical form of Deep Ecology but she teaches more than this. She teaches living the way of the earth—in harmony with it—accepting both life and death and flowing with the changing of the seasons and all of creation "As It Is."

Drahcira is depicted here as being a witch in the best sense of the word. Witchcraft's modern expression as "Wicca" is an earth-based spirituality. It is one of the few religions that truly honors the earth (two exceptions being Native American Spirituality and Creation Spirituality). Its rituals are for the most part based on the changing seasons—the "Wheel of the Year" with its Solstices, Equinoxes and "Quarter Days" in between. And its other rituals follow the cycle of the moon.

Finally I would like to say something about the way this book is put together. The author has used the structure of the Gospels and the Apocalypse as the template for this book. I believe the reason why, is because he is posing in a dramatic way the question, "What if Christ had been a woman?"—a woman whose eyes were focused on the earth rather than heaven?

Ava V. Reich

Part I

The Gospel of the Way of the Earth

"My Ego taught me a new pride, I teach it to you:
No longer to bury your head in the sand of heavenly things,
but carry it freely, an earthly head which
creates meaning for the earth!"
Friedrich Nietzsche

Preface

Forasmuch as none have taken in hand to set forth in order a declaration of those things which are most surely understood among us, it seemed good to me to write this in order that you might know of those things concerning Drahcira, the Prophetess of the Earth.

Chapter I

Now the birth of Drahcira happened this way: There was a virgin engaged to a certain man. One day however another man came to her and said, "You are highly favored and blessed among women!"

2. And when she saw him she was troubled by what he said for she did not know what he meant by such a greeting.

3. Then the man said to her, "Do not be afraid for you have found favor with God. And you will conceive in your womb and bring forth a daughter and she will be great."

4. Then she said to the man, "How shall this be, for I am a virgin?"

5. And the man answered and said to her, "I shall come upon you and my power shall overshadow you therefore that which you shall give birth to shall be called, 'illegitimate!'"

6. And so it was according to his word.

7. Now when the woman began to show that she was pregnant, she arose and hurried into the hill country and entered the house of her aunt. Here she stayed for about three months and then she returned to her house.

8. Now when it was found that she was with child before she and her fiance had come together, he, not wanting to make her a public example decided to put her away secretly. But because of his love for her and having had a dream that made him feel that he should stay with her, he decided to take her as his wife, for that which was conceived within her was not of her choosing.

9. Thus he took her as his wife, though he did not have intercourse with her until she had given birth to her firstborn daughter.

10. And so it was that when it was time for her to give birth, she gave birth to a daughter and called her Drahcira, which by interpretation means, "the way of the earth."

11. And Drahcira grew in both wisdom and stature and in harmony with the earth.

Chapter II

The beginning of the gospel of Drahcira, prophetess of the earth.

2. When Drahcira was about thirty years of age she went into the wilderness in order to learn of herself and the earth. And when she had fasted forty days and forty nights she was famished.

3. And when she was tempted to eat, she stood fast as master of herself and said, "We do not live by bread alone but by the meaning that we give our lives in relation to the whole of the earth. Because rocks are not bread when we wish they were so, does not make them worthless or evil. When we are hungry and there is no food it is not rocks which must change into bread in order for the earth to be good but our thinking which must change in order to adapt to the world 'As It Is'—and our will which must strive to go on despite circumstances."

4. And when she was tempted to think herself deserving of protection from the dangers common to all she said, "It is not good to tempt one's self with such thoughts, for the earth does not revolve around each one of us individually—preparing our ways—making our paths straight and safe. The earth simply is and it is up to us to make our own ways—and when circumstances bring us into danger we must strive not to curse the earth on our account."

5. And when she was tempted by the thought that in the accumulation of wealth and possessions rested the key to fulfillment she said, "We must not yield to the temptation to see

our fulfillment apart from ourselves for it is we who give things their value not things which give us our value."

6. And with this she left the wilderness.

7. And now as Drahcira walked along a certain road she turned and saw two women who were following her and she said to them, "What do you seek?"

8. And they said to her, "Teacher, where do you live?"

9. In reply she simply said, "Come and see." And so it was that they came and saw where she lived and stayed with her that day.

10. One of the two who had followed her, brought her sister to Drahcira. And the next day two others chose to follow her as well. These were the first of Drahcira's disciples.

Chapter III

Now on the third day there was a wedding in a certain town and the mother of Drahcira was there—and Drahcira and her disciples were invited to the wedding reception which followed.

2. And at the reception there were some who abstained from the drinking of wine—looking down upon those who drank. These thought themselves holy for their abstinence.

3. Now when it seemed as if these would ruin this joyous occasion Drahcira's mother said to her, "Speak to the people so that the joy of this occasion is not turned to sadness."

4. And thus spoke Drahcira: "This is a joyous occasion and it is our part to share in the joy of this time with those who have united their lives. There are six barrels here—each holding nearly ten gallons of wine. They are here to make our hearts glad—they are the earth's gift to us which enable us to enter fully, without restraint into the joy of this reception. Let us not spurn the gift which the earth has given us nor the opportunity which these two have given us to share in their joy."

5. And there were none who would openly argue with Drahcira—though some left because of the hardness of their hearts. Thus the reception was once again festive and Drahcira's disciples were amazed at the effect of her words.

Chapter IV

And when Drahcira came upon a town and saw garbage everywhere she said to the people, "Take these things hence for you are making our Mother Earth a dung heap!" And then her disciples remembered that it was written, "Zeal for the earth has eaten her up."

2. Then the people said to her, "What right do you have to say such things to us?"

3. And Drahcira answered and said to them, "The earth has given me this right. And truly I tell you, if we litter the earth it will lose its beauty."

4. And while many ignored her words, there were others who heard her words and believed.

Chapter V

Now there was a certain man—a ruler of the people. This man came to Drahcira by night and said to her, "Miss, we know that you are a teacher come from God for none can say the things you do, except God be with them."

2. And Drahcira answered him saying, "I speak of myself and for the earth. Truly I say to you, unless you awake to the seriousness of our situation, those who follow us—that is our descendants, will never see the earth as it now is!"

3. And the ruler said to her, "How can this be? Will the earth cease to spin or will it plunge from its course and hurl itself into the sun or will it vanish as a vapor?"

4. And Drahcira answered him and said, "How is it that you are a ruler of the people and yet you do not know this? Truly I say unto you, unless you see yourself as a part of the earth and thus live in harmony with it, the earth's fragile balance will be broken and the earth as we know it will be no more, for even now it teeters precariously upon the brink of destruction.

5. "That which is flesh is flesh—and flesh is of the earth. You are not a stranger or pilgrim on this planet—the earth is your home. And thus if your religious beliefs cause you to look upon the earth as fallen and you instead set your sights on heaven, then your beliefs must change. It is not right to let the earth go to hell while you go to your heaven.

6. "How is it that if I spoke to you of heavenly things you would believe me and yet if I speak to you of earthly things you do not believe me? When we sleep we see images which we believe to be real. When we awake however we see things as they really are. Awake! And see the world 'As It Is!'

7. "I have so loved the earth, that I have given it my own life, that whosoever believes my words shall see that in so doing the earth shall not perish but have everlasting life.

8. "I have not come to the world to condemn the world but that the world through my words might be saved. Those who accept my words are not condemned but those who do not are condemned to never truly know the earth as their true home. And this is the condemnation of the world, that the earth offered us its goodness but we scorned it wanting more than what it had to give or what we in our ignorance believed to be better."

Chapter VI

Now as Drahcira walked along the road she came upon a certain place of worship. And now in the heat of the day, being tired from her journey, she came to rest upon its porch.

2. Then a woman came to pray at a time when she knew no others would be likely to come in—for she was known as a prostitute and she dreaded the judgment of others.

3. And Drahcira said to her, "Please get me a drink of water, for I thirst." (Her disciples were away at this time buying food).

4. Then the woman said, "Why are you asking for a drink from me—for I can see you are perfectly able of getting it yourself?"

5. Drahcira answered and said, "There is water to quench my thirst in this place but nothing here will quench that for which you thirst."

6. And the woman said, "Are you greater than God to whom this place is consecrated? Who are you to say that I will not quench my thirst here?"

7. And Drahcira said to her, go call your husband and then we shall settle this."

8. The woman answered and said, "I have no husband."

9. And Drahcira said in return, "You have said well, 'I have no husband' for I understand that you have had five husbands and he who now lives with you is not your husband—in this you have said the truth."

10. With this the woman said, "Could it be that you are a prophetess? My ancestors have sought forgiveness in this place for years and yet you say there is nothing here which will quench my thirst for forgiveness."

11. To this Drahcira replied, "Believe me, the hour is coming when you shall neither in this place nor in another like unto it seek forgiveness. For in truth you have done nothing amiss—unless you so judge. You're so called 'sinfulness' is only so in the minds of those who do not believe you should do as you have done. But what is that to you! You are your own judge and the time is coming, and now is, when you will judge yourself in spirit and truth!"

12. The woman then said, "I know that God will one day judge us all—when He is come, He will tell us all things."

13. Then Drahcira said, "You who speak are the same."

14. And upon this came her disciples and they marveled that she talked with a woman of her reputation, yet none would say, "Why are you talking to her?"

15. Then the woman left and went her way into the city and said to all she met, "Come, see a woman who has shown me a great truth!" Then they went out of the city and came unto her.

16. In the meantime her disciples asked Drahcira to eat the food they had gotten but she said unto them, "I have had food to eat of which you know not." Therefor her disciples said to one another, "Has anyone brought her food to eat?"

17. And Drahcira said to them, "My food is to show others the truth!"

18. And so it was that many people of that city believed Drahcira's words because of the woman. And when they came to Drahcira they asked her if she would stay for a time. And so she stayed there two more days. And many more believed Drahcira's words and thus said to the woman, "Now we believe not because of what you have said but because we have heard Drahcira ourselves and know that her words are true."

Chapter VII

At length Drahcira came again to the city where she had attended the wedding reception. And there was a certain woman whose son was very sick. When she heard that Drahcira had come into town she went and asked her if she would come and heal her son—for he was at the point of death.

2. Then Drahcira said to her, "Except you see signs and wonders you will not believe me."

3. But the woman insisted saying, "Please, come lest my son die!"

4. And thus spoke Drahcira: "I have not come to work miracles in order to change the world 'As It Is' but rather to teach that all must change their way of thinking and accept the way of the earth.

5. "It is written, 'To everything there is a season and a time to every purpose under the heavens: a time to be born and a time to die; a time to plant and a time to reap.' Thus is the way of the earth. It is true that we often wish it were different but our wishing for what is not only increases sorrow.

6. "There is a time to die—all things eventually pass. This is not a matter of our choice but a matter of our acceptance.

7. "I cannot heal your son, Go home and share in his death as you once shared in his birth, for he shall die this very day."

8. And so the woman went home and her son died in her arms that day as Drahcira had said.

Chapter VIII

Then Drahcira came to the town where she had been brought up and she went to the place of worship where she had gone as a child. And there she was given a certain verse of scripture to read.

2. When she read it, it said, "Set your affections on things above, not on things on the earth." And having read this she sat down. And the eyes of all there were fastened upon her.

3. And Drahcira said to them, "These words are written to the hurt of the earth for if you do not set your affections on the earth we will end in destroying it."

4. And all wondered at her words and they said, "Is not this Drahcira, she who was born illegitimately?"

5. Thus she said to them, "You will surely say to me this proverb, 'Physician, heal yourself!' But truly I say to you, rarely is a prophetess accepted in her own town.

6. "I tell you the truth. The scriptures have ministered to your childish dream that the earth should revolve around you. And since it does not, it has promised a place 'Above!' With your affections set on things above, that is on heaven, you are allowing our only true home to waste away through exploitation and neglect."

7. Then when they had all heard these things they were filled with anger and rose up and threw her out and they led her to the brow of the hill upon which their place of worship was built that they might cast her down headlong. But she passed through the midst of them and went on her way.

Chapter IX

And it came to pass that on a certain day as Drahcira taught the people by a lake, many pressed in upon her in order to hear her words. Thus when she saw a boat on the lake she entered into it and asked the owner to push out a little from the shore. And she sat down and taught the people from the boat.

2. Now when she had finished speaking, she asked the owner of the boat if he planned to launch out into the deep in order to fish.

3. And the man answered her saying, "Teacher, I have toiled all night and have taken nothing in, nevertheless at your word I will try again."

4. And Drahcira answered and said to him, "I can see that you respect the earth for you have sustained your life by the fish of its waters. And I sense that though your work has been hard and often disappointing you have never faulted the earth—instead you have persevered. Thus it is that I ask you to follow me and I will make you a fisher of men and women."

5. And straightway he left his boat and followed her.

Chapter X

Then Drahcira entered a certain place and there was a man there who was believed to be possessed by demons. And the man cried out with a loud voice, "Let me alone—what have I to do with you, Drahcira? Have you come here to destroy me? I know who you are—you are the prophetess of the earth!"

2. And Drahcira answered and said to the man, "I have not come to destroy you, I have only come to speak on behalf of the earth. It is said that what obsesses or possesses you is evil or even demonic."

3. And then turning to the others who were there she said, "There are none of us here who have perfect command of our minds or emotions. All of us are troubled by various fears which express themselves in diverse ways. And all are as well ignorant of much of the vast dimensions of our minds with their unfathomable depths. Thus, we too can have our own obsessions and we can even be possessed by thoughts of gaining that which we obsess about.

4. "Therefore, rather than fear this man—believing him to be possessed by demons, we must determine to show compassion for him who is less fortunate than we ourselves.

5. "What is done with this man must be decided in view of the possible danger he poses to others as well as to himself.

6. "Can I heal this man? I can only perform a healing ritual." And so she began by arranging an altar on a large rock by a stream near to them. And on it she put symbols of the four elements. To

the East she put a feather that was upon the ground as a symbol of the element of air and to the South she lit some sage in an earthen bowl. To the West she set another earthen bowl of water drawn from the stream and to the North she put a stone the size of one's palm on the rock. Then she put a piece of the man's clothes on the altar as well.

7. Then Drahcira cleansed the circle of the area and the man with sage; wafting the sweet smelling herb about the man and around the area in which the ritual was to be performed.

8. And then, speaking so all could hear she said, "We now exercise power and authority over whatever evil is disturbing this man and we banish it to a place of outer darkness! So mote it be!" And from that moment the man began to heal.

9. Then Drahcira said to those who had witnessed this ritual, "And now let us therefore, as one, take this man to a place where he can be cared for and let us carry his burden as we would for one of our own loved ones. In peace we have come; in peace we now part. Blessed be!"

10. And so they took the man away and he was cared for at the expense of all those who had heard Drahcira's words, for he had no family of his own.

Chapter XI

And then, when she had left that place she entered into the house of one of her disciples.

2. And her disciple's father-in-law was there and he mocked Drahcira saying, "You labor in vain for no one's words can save the earth for it is sick unto death!"

3. And Drahcira came and took him by the hand. And looking steadfast into his eyes she said to him, "It is true that the earth is sick but it has not yet been determined whether her sickness is unto death. The earth has surely been injured but injuries do heal and with their healing they bring scars—the flesh of which is tougher than the original tissue.

4. "It is true that we cannot turn back the hands of time—nor can we undo that which has been done. And thus while the earth is not sick unto death, it is true that the earth as we know it is!

5. "Therefore I teach repentance—that is to say, that all would change their way of thinking and embrace the earth as both Mother and home. And while it is in no wise certain that those to whom I speak will give heed to my words—still I must speak words which the earth has given me."

6. And immediately he repented of his words and ministered unto Drahcira.

7. And at evening, when the sun did set, they brought unto Drahcira all that were in need of such repentance. And thus the entire town gathered together at the door. And the minds of many were changed for the good of the earth and thus for the good of all living things.

Chapter XII

And it came to pass that the next morning, rising up a great while before dawn, Drahcira went out to a solitary place and there she communed with herself.

2. And her disciples, not knowing where she had gone searched for her. And when they had found her they said to her, "Teacher, why did you leave without telling us where you would be?"

3. And she said, "How is it that you have sought me? Did you not know that I must be about my own affairs? And now, let us go into the next town that I may teach there also—for thus have I come."

4. And so Drahcira went about that region teaching all the gospel of the way of the earth.

5. And her fame spread and there followed her great crowds of people from those places where she had taught.

Chapter XIII

And it came to pass, when she was in a certain city she saw a diabetic who had lost both of his legs. And he fell on his face before her saying, "Teacher, if the way of the earth is good, then why does it take such grievous turns and commit such acts of cruelty as in my own affliction?"

2. And Drahcira, moved with compassion, put forth her hand and touched him saying, "Is the earth not good if fire burns or serpents strike? Or should we consider the earth cruel because hearts fail or diseases come upon us?

3. "It is true that we do not like such things and that we experience such things as cruel but our experience does not make them so. The earth is not cruel for she does not act with intent rather she operates according to natural laws. Thus your affliction is simply the way of the earth.

4. "Misfortunes such as your own, rather than serving as a cause for cursing the earth should instead serve both as a motivation for you to live creatively by your will and to show compassion for others. In any case, your part now must be to accept your world "As It Is" rather than suffer doubly by wishing your world were different."

5. And as soon as she had spoken, immediately the man's self-pity left him and he accepted his lot.

6. And Drahcira said to him, "Go and repeat this teaching to others who are similarly afflicted."

7. And so the man left and began to share this teaching with many.

Chapter XIV

Now after some days news spread that Drahcira had entered a certain house and many were gathered together—so many that there was no room to receive them all. And Drahcira taught those who were in the house and gathered about the doorway.

2. And a young woman came who had heard of Drahcira's message and perceived the truth of it. This same young woman longed to hear Drahcira herself.

3. And when she could not find a way to enter the house she went upon the housetop and had a friend help her remove some tiles and let her down into the house before Drahcira.

4. And when Drahcira saw the young woman's determination she said to her, "Daughter, you have damaged the roof of this house in your zeal to hear the truth—woe be to those who damage the earth and the life therein while selfishly ignoring the truth!"

5. And certain of those who were in that house began to reason among themselves saying, "Who is Drahcira to justify the damaging of an other's property?"

6. And immediately when Drahcira heard what they were saying she said to them, "Which is easier—to repair this roof or to make whole the earth and those who have been hurt through selfishness?

7. "But that you may know which is the greater evil (she said to the young woman)—arise and go to your home for you have

received the truth and it is thus no more needful that you be instructed by me."

8. And immediately the young woman arose and went forth before them all and Drahcira paid for the repair of the roof from her own means.

9. And all were amazed and said, "We have seen a strange thing this day."

Chapter XV

After this there was a religious festival in a nearby town and Drahcira decided to go to it.

2. Now there was in this town a pool of water called "The Pool of Mercy" which had five porches. And during this festival many would come to this pool in order to be ritually cleansed of their sins.

3. And a certain man was there who had come to the festival every year for thirty eight years and yet had never been able to enter the pool because of the crowds.

4. When Drahcira saw the man she said to him, "Would you like to be cleansed?"

5. And the man said to her, "All of these years I have never been able to enter the pool because of the crowds."

6. Then Drahcira said to him, "This water is no different than any other—it can cleanse the filthiness of the flesh but it can do nothing for one's inner self.

7. "And the cleansing of one's inner self is something which is altogether unnecessary, rather we must forget those things which are past for they no longer are, and determine to live true to ourselves in the present—irrespective of the expectations of others.

8. "Therefore I say to you, leave this place for that which you seek will not be found here but rather within yourself!"

9. And immediately the man saw himself anew and thus he left the area that surrounded the pool.

10. Now when certain of the devotees who attended this religious festival saw the man leaving the area surrounding the pool they said to him, "Why are you leaving this holy festival? Have you no need to be cleansed of your sins?"

11. He said that Drahcira had told him to leave for she said that the waters of this pool can cleanse nothing more than the filthiness of the flesh.

12. Then Drahcira said, "I have only spoken the truth. Search your scriptures—in them you think you have the way to eternal life but their words are only the expression of the longings of those who have never accepted the world "As It Is"—nor themselves. Hear rather the way of the earth which I teach.

13. And with that these devotees left determined to persecute Drahcira for she taught contrary to their beliefs and made of naught their festival and its "Pool of Mercy."

Chapter XVI

Now after these things it came to pass that Drahcira walked through an apple orchard on the Sabbath day and her disciples, being hungry, began to pick the apples and eat them.

2. And there were those who thought themselves holy nearby who saw this and said to Drahcira, "What your disciples are doing is not lawful on the Sabbath. The Sabbath is a day of rest wherein we are commanded to refrain from working and yet you have allowed your disciples to harvest apples and thus profane the holy Sabbath day."

3. And Drahcira answered them saying, "Do the priests profane the Sabbath day? For they do their work in the places of worship every Sabbath. But in this they are held blameless for you see that what they do must be done. Necessity sometimes commands us to do contrary to those commandments which are held to be sacred.

4. "And if it is lawful for us to take from the air our breath that we might breathe on the Sabbath, why do we err in taking from the earth its fruit that it might sustain us?

5. "In your zeal to observe the law strictly you have forgotten that this law was given to bless not curse—to give rest not force us into inactivity. The Sabbath was made for you and not you for the Sabbath. Therefore it is we who are Lords over the Sabbath!"

6. And with this Drahcira left with her disciples and entered a certain place of worship. But those who had seen the disciples picking apples and had heard Drahcira's words ran ahead. And they

told those who were there that, "Drahcira teaches contrary to our commandments!"

7. And when Drahcira heard what was said concerning her she said to them, "What person among you having a child—if your child fell into a pit on the Sabbath day would leave him or her there until the sun set? Would you not rather pull your child out of the pit? If then it is good to pick a child out of a pit that their day be not spent in suffering, why then would it be evil if one picked and apple from a tree that one's day be not spent in hunger?

8. "Truly I say to you, in your zeal to observe the law perfectly you have failed to see that perfection comes not from conforming to commandments printed in a book but rather in conforming to the way of the earth."

9. Then those who thought themselves holy went out and held council against her that they might be rid of her.

Chapter XVII

And it came to pass that a large crowd followed Drahcira. And seeing the crowd she went up on a mountain and sat down. And the crowd sat before her.

2. And she taught the people saying, "Blessed are those of a teachable spirit for they shall learn.

"Blessed are the poor of material things for they have the occasion to know their value apart from possessions.

"Blessed are those who mourn for they shall know how to comfort.

"Blessed are those who live simply for they are the friends of the earth.

"Blessed are those who hunger and thirst for understanding for they shall be filled.

"Blessed are the clear of sight for they shall see the world 'As It Is.'

"Blessed are the peacemakers for they labor that harmony might reign.

"Blessed are the merciful for they are able to accept others in spite of their faults.

"Blessed are you when others shall revile you and persecute you and shall say all manner of evil against you falsely. Instead rejoice and be glad for your reward will be in knowing that you have defended the defenseless earth and have spoken on behalf of that which cannot speak.

3. "But woe to you who are rich for danger lies in not valuing yourselves apart from your possessions.

And woe to you who hunger and thirst after 'the world-to-come,' for you shall never know 'the world-as-it-is.'

And woe to you who compromise yourselves in order to gain the favor of others for in so doing you betray yourselves as well as those whom you seek to impress.

4. "We are the caretakers of the earth but if the caretakers abandon their vocation, how shall the earth be cared for? And herein lies the 'sin' of the caretakers: that not only do they not care for the earth but they exploit and pollute it beyond imagining.

5. "We are the light of the world. A city that is set on a hill cannot be hid. Neither do we light a candle and put it under a bowl but rather we put it on a candle stand and thus it lights the room. Therefore let your light shine in the world that all may see your good works and thus be moved to accept the earth 'As It Is.'

6. "Think not that I have come to destroy your faith in God—I have not come to destroy it but rather to build your faith in the earth. For truly I say to you, many gods have come and gone and yet the earth has remained. Therefore whoever hurts the earth and teaches others to do so shall be called an enemy of the earth. But whoever helps the earth and teaches others to do so shall be called a friend of the earth. For truly I tell you, unless your zeal for the earth shall exceed that of the religious devotee's zeal for their religion you will not experience the way of the earth.

7. "You have heard that it was said by those of times past that 'Whoever is angry with another without cause shall be in danger of the judgment and whoever calls another a fool shall be in danger of hell-fire.' But I say to you that whenever we are angry with another person for whatever cause, the anger is not evil of itself but is simply part of what it is to be human. And the only judgment we shall face will be the judgment which falls between us on account of our anger. And when we feel moved to call another person a fool we would do well to ask first if we have not done and said foolish things ourselves. Truly I say to you, the only hell which awaits us

is that which we create ourselves through our hurtful words and deeds.

8. "You have heard that it was said by those of times past that 'Whoever looks upon a woman with lust has already committed adultery with her in their hearts.' And furthermore it was said, 'If your eyes offend you, pluck them out for it is better to lose one's eyes than to be cast into hell.' But I say to you that these words are not true for our attraction to others is the way of the earth.

9. "It has been said that 'Whoever divorces and remarries commits adultery.' But I say these words are only based on religious tradition. In the way of the earth some animals and birds mate for life while others do not—and yet both behave according to their natures. Do our natures bind us to one alone for life? Yes, for many but not for all.

10. "Again you have heard that it was said by those of times past concerning the making of vows. 'Let your communication be simply yes or no for whatever is more comes of evil.' But I say to you that all have the right to make whatever vow they so choose and if circumstances change wherein the vow must be broken, there is no 'sin' in this for a vow is not a moral laws but a stated intention.

11. "You have heard that it has been said, 'Resist not evil but whoever slaps you on your right cheek, turn to them the other also.' But I say to you, resist evil for whatever you allow to be done you are in that case condoning.

12. "You have heard that it has been said, 'Love your enemies for your Father in heaven makes his sun rise on the evil and the good and sends rain on the just and the unjust.' But I say to you that as soon as you look upon another as your enemy you will not be able to love them. As the sun and rain make no difference with whom they share their treasures, we would do well to learn the way of the earth and thus learn to share our love impartially. Therefore be even as the earth is.

13. "There is only one earth, and we are her prophets.

14. "So when you are moved to commune with the earth, commune like this:

'O Earth our home—
Holy be your name.
Your plant and animal kingdoms yet endure—
Thus let you will be done
As it was in times past.
Give us this day our daily bread
And forgive us where we have failed you
Even as we forgive those who have failed us.
And let us not be led to betray you
But deliver us from such temptations.
For you are our home and our sustenance—
May we thus honor you forever.
Blessed be!'

15. And when you give alms, do not do it in order to be praised of others, rather do it in secret simply because you know it is right.

16. And when you fast, do not do it in order to be praised of others, rather do it to purge your body of impurities—and do this too in secret simply because you feel it is what you need to you.

17. And be sure that you make pilgrimages at least once a year out into nature—to be in the rivers, oceans, forests, mountains, meadows and even the deserts. It will be well for you.

18. "Lay not up for yourselves treasures in heaven, which may not even exist, but rather see the earth as your treasure. For where your treasure is there will your heart be also. The hope of the earth lies in our loyalty. If therefore our loyalty be divided, the earth as we have known it, shall not endure. No one can serve two masters for either you will hate the one and love the other or else you will hold to one and despise the other. You cannot serve the earth while exploiting and polluting it.

19. "Therefore I say to you, take thought of your life—what you shall eat and what you shall drink and how you shall live. But what is more important than these is that our way of life does not prevent the birds of the air and the trees that they dwell in or all of the plants and all of the creatures of the earth from living as they have right to. Seek first to live in harmony with the way of the

earth and all the rest will be as it should be. And thus it is that we must take thought for the future, for the future shall not take care of itself. What we do today will affect the earth and all that dwell upon it tomorrow.

20. "It is impossible not to judge another but be mindful of this, that in judging we most often read our own past into another. And thus we do not see them as they are but rather as we imagine them to be. Thus how is it that you behold a splinter in an other's eye but do not realize that there is a beam in your own eye? First cast the beam out of your own eye and then you will see clearly the other's eye.

21. "Do not force your views upon those who do not want to receive them, lest they turn upon you.

22. "Ask that you might learn. Seek, and you will find. Knock, and the way will be opened for you. For those who ask with an open mind shall learn and those who seek will find and those who knock—the doors will open for them.

23. "All things that you would want others to do for you, do so even for them for such is the law of giving and receiving.

24. "Enter in at the broad gate, for narrow is the gate and straight is the way that leads to heaven—this is, in the minds of those who think themselves holier than you. But broad is the gate and wide is the way of life which lies ever before us.

25. "Beware of false prophets who come to you in sheep's clothing for they are more like ravening wolves. You shall know them by their fruit. Do we gather grapes of thorn bushes or figs of thistles?—of course not! The message of a false prophet will either bring hurt to the earth or belittle it in an effort to show the 'world-to-come' as our 'true' home. The message of the true prophet however will bring healing to the earth and show it to be not only our home but our Mother and that for which we are responsible as her caretakers.

26. "Not everyone who calls me Teacher shall know the way of the earth but rather, only those who follow its path. Many will one day say to me, 'Teacher, we have taught that which you have taught us and through your instruction have done many good things.'

And then I will say to them, 'You have done well and thus the earth rejoices with me at your labor of love!' Therefore whoever will learn of the earth and also live in harmony with it I liken to a wise person who built their house upon a rock. For when the rain poured down and the floods came it did not fall for it was founded on a rock. But everyone who will not learn of the earth nor live in harmony with it I liken to a foolish person who built their house on the sand. For when the rain poured down and the floods came it fell—and great was the fall of it."

27. "And it came to pass, when Drahcira had ended these sayings that the people were astonished at her teachings for she taught them as one having authority and not as those who thought themselves holy and speculated concerning the "world-to-come."

28. And when she came down from the mountain many followed her.

Chapter XVIII

Now when Drahcira entered a certain town a soldier came to her and asked her, "Teacher, my friend lies at home paralyzed from the waist down as a result of the war. More than this, he has given up the will to live for he now sees his life as meaningless."

2. And Drahcira said, "I will come you and visit your friend."

3. Now when Drahcira came to the man's house she spoke to the man saying, "I know that you grieve the loss of your legs and that your grief is more than you can bear. But does one's life consist of more than one's legs?

4. "When one grieves, one's eyes become focused on nothing more than the object of one's grief and yet there is much more to be seen. Be not like a horse who wearing blinders can look neither to the right nor to the left. You must remove your blinders and see that your life consists of more than your legs.

5. "More than this, you must see the meaning of your life not in your legs nor even in your life as you wish it would be but rather in the world as a whole and the place you fill here. For none of us can live wholly to ourselves, but rather we live in relation to the whole of the earth."

6. Then he who was paralyzed answered and said to Drahcira, "Teacher, I am not worthy that you should be under my roof. But speak the word only and I will do as you say—for I was once a soldier who acted under authority, and I had soldiers under me as

well. And I said to this man Come' and he came and to another 'Go' and he went, and to another 'Do this' and he did it."

7. When Drahcira heard this she was amazed and said to those who followed her, "Truly I say to you, I have not seen such a change in someone in all of my days."

8. And then, turning to him who was paralyzed she said, "Remove the blinders of grief from your eyes and now see the meaning of your life as part of the whole of the earth 'As It Is.'"

9. And the soldier let go of his grief that very day.

Chapter XIX

And it came to pass on the next day that Drahcira set forth for another town and her disciples went with her as well as many others. Now when she came close to the border of the town there was a dead child being carried out—the only daughter of a widow—and there were many with her.

2. And when Drahcira saw her she had compassion on her and said to her, "Weep on, for as the rain which falls cleanses the sky of impurities, so do your tears purge your soul of your great loss. But as the rain does not wash away the earth itself but rather nourishes it, so your tears will not wash away the memory of your daughter but rather they shall bind your lives together in such a way that you shall never forget her.

3. "More than this, a part of your daughter has become incarnate within you. In your mind you still see her face—you still hear her voice—you still feel her touch. And thus she shall ever be with you so long as you live for she is a part of you."

4. And with these words Drahcira embraced the woman and kissed her saying, "Weep on, for now is the season of rain and the seasons of the earth must surely come—it is the way of the earth."

5. And there came fear on many for they said, "Who is this prophetess who speaks not of the 'world-to-come'?" And this rumor of her spread throughout the region and beyond.

Chapter XX

Then she began to rebuke the cities where she had labored but which continued in ways harmful to the earth.

2. "Woe to you! For if you do not repent of your ways the earth as we have known it will cease to exist. Even now both the air and water are polluted. Even now the earth is warming and the ice caps and glaciers are melting. And myriads of species have already ceased to exist. Yes, the earth will go on but without our descendants.

3. "But to those of every city who do repent—be they ever so few, I say, come to me all you who labor on behalf of the earth and we will rest together. And then refreshed, we shall yoke ourselves together and thus labor in union. But know this: my yoke is not easy and my burden is not light."

Chapter XXI

And it came to pass that one of those who thought herself holy asked Drahcira to come to her house and eat with her. And so she went to this pious woman's house and sat down to eat.

2. And when a woman in that city who was of questionable character knew that Drahcira had sat down to eat in the pious woman's house, she brought an alabaster vase filled with fragrant oil and stood behind her. And when Drahcira turned in her seat the woman knelt down and took off Drahcira's shoes and began to massage her feet with the oil she brought. And when she was done she wiped her feet with the hair of her head and then she kissed her feet.

3. Now when the pious woman who had invited Drahcira saw this she said to her, "If you were truly a prophetess you would know what kind of woman this is who touches you—for she is a sinner!"

4. And Drahcira said to the pious woman, "I have something to ask you. How is it that we are made of flesh and blood?"

5. And she said, "It is God who made us so!"

6. Then Drahcira said, "And does your God create evil and shameful things or those things which are good and perfect?"

7. And the pious woman said, "It is written that all that God has created is good!"

8. Therefore Drahcira said to the woman, "Then you must agree that our bodies are good and that there is nothing shameful about them. Surely your God would not create shameful things.

And more than this, these same bodies have been made in such a way that they sense pleasure—and this woman who you call a 'sinner' lives to bring pleasure to those who desire it. Because she is able to do this with another does this make her evil?"

9. And the pious woman said, "It is not evil that she brings pleasure to others but that she sins in transgressing the laws of God!"

10. And thus spoke Drahcira: "What you believe to be the laws of God are on this earth nothing more than the commandments of men. For if it cannot be proven that your God exists neither can it be proven that the laws you ascribe to him are true. Here on this earth, what you call the laws of God are such only to those who believe in your God. And this woman, whom you call a 'sinner' because of your beliefs, could serve as a priestess in the temple of a Goddess because those who attend there hold different beliefs. More than this, many acts which you would call abominations such as a man lying with a man or a woman with a woman are seen as perfectly natural according to the way of the earth.

11. Then Drahcira turned to the woman and said to the pious woman, "Do you see this woman? When I entered your house you gave me no kiss and yet this woman has kissed my feet. And while your false piety has brought only sadness, her hands have brought me pleasure. Therefore I say to you, her 'sins' which you believe are many are such only in your mind—just as your holiness which you believe to be great is also only in your mind."

12. Then Drahcira said to the 'sinful' woman, "Go in peace for it is you who are truly holy in that you are not ashamed of the way of the earth and more than this, you follow it rather than the commandments of men."

13. And when it was heard what Drahcira had said, those who thought themselves to be holy began to say among themselves, "Who is this that calls the laws of God the commandments of men?"

Chapter XXII

And it came to pass afterward that Drahcira went throughout the cities and villages teaching the gospel of the way of the earth. And her disciples were with her as well as certain men who helped to support the work of Drahcira and her disciples.

2. And they went into a certain house and a large crowd gathered. And they brought to her one who could not see the truth of Drahcira's message. But when Drahcira, through her teachings gave the man his sight, those who thought themselves holy said, "This woman is blind and therefore leads the blind! And this man who says he now can see the truth of Drahcira's message has in truth been made blind by Drahcira's words—for she speaks the words of the Devil!"

3. But Drahcira answered saying, "Every kingdom that speaks against itself is brought down and every city or house that speaks against itself shall fall. And if I were to teach your message of the 'world-to-come' would I not thereby speak against the world 'As It Is.' Thus in teaching your message I would be laboring to bring hurt to the earth. For if what is of ultimate value is your 'world-to-come' what is to prevent us from ignoring the needs of the earth 'As It Is' and the delicate balance that is needed for all that is herein?'

4. "Those who are not in accord with this message bring hurt to the earth and those who do not gather with me are scattering abroad. Therefore I say to you, all manner of 'sin' and blasphemy

can be forgiven but to 'sin' against the earth is to blaspheme our Mother and home.

5. "O generation of vipers, how can you being self-centered speak of things which will benefit the earth—for out of the abundance of the heart the mouth speaks. Self-centered people, out of the treasure of their hearts bring forth those things which are fit for themselves while those who are one with the earth bring forth those things which are fit for the whole of the earth."

6. Then certain of those who were in that place said, "Teacher, we would like to see a sign from you." But she said to them, "A superstitious people look for signs but no sign shall be given to you other than what I have taught before—that even now both the air and water are polluted, and the earth is warming and the ice caps and glaciers are melting. Myriads of species have already ceased to exist and many more are lost to the earth every day. What more signs do you need from me than these?"

7. And while she spoke someone said to Drahcira that her mother was outside and desired to speak to her. She said that she would speak to her when she had finished her teachings. In the meantime however she said to the crowd, "Who is my mother?" And she stretched forth her hand towards the earth and said, "Behold my Mother." And then stretching forth her hand to her disciples and said, "And behold my brothers and sisters. For all those who do the will of my Mother the earth are my brothers and sisters."

8. Then one in the house said, "Teacher, speak to my brother that he should divide his inheritance with me."

9. And she said to him, "Who made me a judge over you? A person's life does not consist of the abundance of things which he possesses."

10. And she told them a parable saying, "A certain man inherited a large sum of money as well as many things. And so the man thought, 'What shall I do because I have no room where I can keep all of these things?' So he said, 'This I will do. I will build a great storage shed and there I will keep all of my things. Then will I say, 'You have enough money and things now laid up

for many years. Take your ease—eat, drink and be merry.' But that very night he died. Thus I ask you, what value are all of his things to him in the grave? Therefore, having food and shelter, let us therewith be content."

Chapter XXIII

The same day Drahcira went out of the house and sat by the water. And a great crowd gathered together to hear her, so she got into a boat and began to teach many things using parables saying,

2. "A sower went out to sow. And when she sowed some seed fell by the wayside and the birds of the air ate them.

3. "And some fell upon stony ground where there was not much earth but they grew quickly. But when the sun was hot they died and withered away because they had no roots.

4. "And some fell among the thorns—and the thorns sprung up and choked them.

5. "But others fell into good ground and brought forth an abundance of fruits and vegetables.

Those who have ears to hear, let them hear."

6. And the people said to her, "Why do you speak to us in parables?"

7. And she answered and said to them, "I speak in parables because seeing you see not and hearing you hear not—neither do you understand. And thus I use them that you may see, hear and understand the world 'As It Is.' Blessed are those of you who are willing to learn. For truly I say to you that there are many who do not desire to see those things which I am showing you—nor hear those things of which I speak. Hear therefore the meaning of the parable of the sower.

8. "When any one hears the gospel of the way of the earth and understands it not, then others come and snatch away that which was sown in the heart. These are they who received seed by the wayside.

9. "And those who received the seed upon stony ground, the same are they who hear the word and receive it with joy, yet having no roots endure for but a while. For when trouble or even persecution comes they give up.

10 "They also who received seed among the thorns are they who hear the word but the cares of life and lure of riches choke the word which was sown in the heart and thus they become unfruitful.

11. "But those who received seed in the good ground are they who hear the word and understand it—and thus bring forth an abundance of fruit."

12. Another parable she shared saying, "The world 'As It Is' is like a woman who sowed good seed in her field but it came to pass when the blades sprung up and brought forth fruit so did weeds appear.

13. "So the children of the woman came and said to her, 'Mother, did you not sow good seed in our field?' And the mother said, 'Yes I did.' Then they asked her, 'Why then are there weeds in our field?' And she said to them, 'The weeds come from the earth and they belong here just as much as our crops do.' Then the children said, 'But shouldn't we pluck the weeds so they don't destroy our crops?' Thus said the mother, 'We must do, what we must do in order to sustain ourselves, but know this—just as we pluck up the weeds and they then die so some day we too shall be plucked up and thus shall die.'

"Those who have ears to hear, let them hear."

14. And another parable she shared with the people saying, "The message I bring is like a grain of mustard seed, which a woman took and sowed in her field. And though it is one of the smallest seeds, when it is grown it becomes a place where even the birds of the air may nest. Or it is like yeast, which a woman took and put into dough and it rose to become a loaf of bread."

15. Then Drahcira said, "When one learns the gospel of the way of the earth it is like a treasure buried in a field, which when one finds it, he would gladly sell everything that he had in order to obtain the field and thus have the treasure. Or it is like a merchant seeking pearls, who when he finds one of great price, he goes and sells all that he has and buys it."

16. And Drahcira said unto them, "Have you understood all these things?" And they said to her, "Yes, we have." And with this Drahcira left that place.

Chapter XXIV

Before they launched out for the other side of the lake a certain man came to her and said, "Teacher, I will follow you wherever you go."

2. And Drahcira said to him, "The foxes have their holes in the earth and the birds have their nests in the trees—surely the earth reserves a place for us to lay our heads as well."

3. Then one of her disciples said to her, "Teacher, allow me to go bury my father."

4. And Drahcira said to her, "We will wait for you for the dead cannot bury themselves. And it is good that your father be returned to the earth from whence he came."

5. And so Drahcira and the others waited for her disciple to return. And when she did they entered into the boat and launched out for the other side of the lake.

6. But as they sailed Drahcira fell asleep while a great storm arose. And though the boat was covered by the waves, Drahcira slept on.

7. And her disciples came to her and awoke her saying, "Teacher, save us or we will all perish!"

8. But Drahcira said to them, "If we perish, we perish. Our part now while we yet live is to keep our wits about us and ride out the storm. The storm shall pass and we shall live by our will to overcome."

9. And when they had labored long in the middle of the storm, it finally abated. And her disciples were amazed at what manner of people they were becoming that even the winds and the waves could not overcome them.

Chapter XXV

And when they came to the other side, there they met a certain ascetic you lived among the tombs. And always, night and day he was in the mountains and among the tombs crying and cutting himself with stones.

2. But when he saw Drahcira he fell down before her and with a loud voice said, "Teacher, which is the true way—yours or mind? For I come neither eating and drinking and despising the flesh and they say I have a demon. While you come both eating and drinking—taking pleasure in the flesh and they say you are a glutton and a drunkard."

3. And thus spoke Drahcira: "Let 'them' say whatever they want—what is that to us—for they speak out of ignorance. What they say is of no importance but 'which is the true way' is indeed of great importance. Your way is according to your nature but it is not according to the way of the earth for the earth made us in such a way that we may take pleasure in the flesh. We have senses for the enjoyment of the earth—we can look upon its beauty, smell its fragrances, taste of its fruits and feel the pleasurable sensations of the body.

4. "You however feel wrong in doing so. This feeling of wrongness stems from two sources: First as an error in thinking—that is, thinking that the earth and the flesh are inherently evil while the 'world-to-come' and the spirit are good. The second is your experience of guilt—which also comes from your belief that

the flesh is evil. See the earth and the flesh as good—accept the world 'As It Is' and the experience of guilt will leave you and thus your need to punish yourself. Furthermore, this is not a matter of your way or my way but rather your way or the way of the earth."

5. And when they went into town and sat down to eat in a certain inn, the people saw the ascetic sitting with Drahcira and her disciples eating and drinking and the people were amazed!

6. And when they returned to their boat he who had been an ascetic said that he wanted to go with them. But Drahcira said to him, "Go back to your town and tell the people what you have learned."

7. And the man went back and told all that he met what he had learned.

8. And Drahcira and her disciples got back into the boat and sailed over and came to her own city.

Chapter XXVI

And it came to pass, as Drahcira sat and ate at a certain house many 'sinful' people came and sat down with Drahcira and her disciples. And when those who thought themselves holy saw it they said to her disciples, "Why does your teacher eat with sinners?"

2. But when Drahcira heard this she said to them, "They who are whole do not need a physician but they who are sick. And it is you rather than these that need a physician!"

3. Then they answered her saying, "We cannot accept your teachings for you speak falsely and not according to the words of our fathers!"

4. Then Drahcira told them a parable: "No one sews a piece of new cloth on an old garment for the new piece will shrink when washed and tear away from the old, making the tear worse. Neither do people put new wine into old wine skins, for the old skin will burst when the wine ferments and thus the wine must be put into new wine skins so that they will grow together."

Chapter XXVII

Then a leader of a certain place of worship came to Drahcira and fell at her feet and said to her, "My daughter has died and I would like you to commit her body to the earth."

2. And so it was that Drahcira went with the man and many people followed.

3. And a certain woman who had been bleeding for twelve years, and had suffered many things of many physicians, and had spent all that she had and had not gotten better but rather grew worse—when she heard Drahcira she said in her heart, "If I may but touch her I will be whole." And so she came in among the people and touched her.

4. And immediately she stopped bleeding and she felt in her body that she had been healed.

5. And Drahcira turned and said, "Who touched me?"

6. And her disciples said to her, "You see how many people are here and you say, 'Who touched me?'"

7. And Drahcira looked around to see who had done this. But the woman came forward and told Drahcira, in front of all of the people, why she had touched her and how she had been healed.

8. And Drahcira said to her, "Though a woman's blood is good and not evil, it is not good for this cleansing flow to bleed continually for then one cannot conceive and give birth as the earth intends. Be glad and know this, that it was not me who healed you but your own faith that made you whole. Because you

believed unwaveringly that in touching me you would be healed, your mind—whose powers are unfathomable—did that which no physician could do. It restored wholeness. Thus it was not the object of your belief that brought you healing but the belief itself. Therefore go now in peace and in wholeness."

9. And when Drahcira came to the place where the girl was to be buried, and when she saw those who wept she said to them, "Though it is a hard thing to lose one we love, thus it is. And now the earth from whence she came shall receive her unto itself once more—'for dust we are and unto dust shall we return.'"

10. And filling her hands with the earth which had been dug from the girl's grave, Drahcira said, "Sleep on daughter of the earth." And spreading the earth over the girl she said, "I spread this earth over you as your father once spread your blanket upon you as you rested at night. And now your body will become one with the earth and your spirit will go where we cannot follow. Now you will join those who have gone before you and now you go before us. And that which remains a mystery to us is now reality to you. Sleep on fair child for in sleep there is no pain—and may your dreams be forever sweet. So mote it be—blessed be!"

Chapter XXVIII

And when Drahcira left that place three men followed her saying, "Teacher, tell us, what is 'The Truth'?"

2. And when she entered a certain house Drahcira said to the men, "Do you believe that I am able to show you this?" And they said to her, "Yes Teacher, we do."

3. And thus spoke Drahcira: "That which is said to be 'The Truth' must be of such a nature that it can be shown to be such to all. If it cannot be proven to be true, then it is rather and opinion or belief which may or may not be true. If for example I say, 'Fire is hot' this can be shown to be true for all—young and old, male and female, rich and poor—and those of every nation, kindred and tongue will see the truth of these words as well. If however I say, 'Hell is hot'—though there be many who hold this as truth, there is no way it can be shown to be true and thus we see that it can therefore only be held as an opinion or belief."

4. But the men questioned among themselves concerning the value of this teaching.

5. And so it was that Drahcira said to them, "The value of this teaching is that no more can one persecute another for the sake of 'The Truth.' For those things which can be shown to be true are such that one would not fight for them. Rather they are only opinions and beliefs, mistakenly held as truths which are imposed or defended by force by those who hold them. Once these 'Truths' are seen to be what they are, the folly of imposing or defending

them will become clear. For the sake of all, truth must be separated from opinion and belief. Opinions and beliefs must no longer be allowed to masquerade as 'The Truth'!"

6. And when the men left they mocked this teaching for they cherished their beliefs as truths.

7. But there was in that same house a woman who had listened to Drahcira's words to these men. And when she went out she spread her teaching. And many marveled at the simplicity of the truth saying, "Never was it so taught in this place!" But those who thought themselves holy said, "Drahcira speaks lies of the Father of Lies!"—that is to say, the Devil—who also is just a belief.

Chapter XXIX

And she left and came to her home town. And her disciples were with her.

2. And when the Sabbath day came, she began to teach in a certain place and many hearing her were amazed, saying, "Where did this Drahcira gain such wisdom? Isn't she the carpenter's daughter? Isn't Nasus, her mother? And aren't her brothers and sisters with us?" And they were offended by her.

3. But Drahcira said to them, "A Prophetess is not without honor except in her own town and among her own people."

4. And thus she could do little to turn their hearts towards the way of the earth for they had closed their minds to her.

Chapter XXX

And Drahcira went about all the cities, towns and villages teaching the gospel of the way of the earth. But when she saw the people, she was moved with compassion for them.

2. Then she said to her disciples, "There are many who are ready to learn the way of the earth but the teachers are few. We need more to teach the way of the earth."

3. Then she called her disciples together and said to them, "Go your ways. I am sending you out into the world. In whatever house you enter, first say, 'Peace be upon this house.' And if you are invited to stay there eat and drink what is served to you. And into whatever city you enter and they are open to you, teach them the gospel of the way of the earth. But into whatever city you enter and they are not open to you—be on your way, for it is fruitless to speak to those who do not want to listen and to teach those who do not want to learn.

4. Be wise as owls and harmless as doves. And beware of those who think themselves holy, for they will denounce you before all. But when they do, take no thought of what you shall say, for it will come to you that same hour what you must say. Truly I say to you, as long as you are centered in yourself and in the earth, you will know what must be said.

5. "Do not fear those who speak evil of you, for their words cannot hurt you, neither can they change the truth of the earth 'As It Is.' Therefore speak the truth as you must and do not fear them.

We have come in peace but because they feel they must defend their 'truth' (which in truth is only belief which may or may not be true) they may persecute you as the destroyers of 'The Truth.'"

6. And it came to pass that when Drahcira finished her instructions to her disciples they left and went to many places teaching the gospel of the way of the earth.

Chapter XXXI

And when at length her disciples returned, they told her all that they had done. And she said to them, "Let us go to a place where we can be alone and eat and rest for a while"—for there were many coming and going and they had no time to even eat.

2. And so they went into a solitary place. But the people kept looking for them and soon found them.

3. And Drahcira said to them, "Have you not read, 'To everything there is a season and a time to every purpose under the heavens?' Truly I say to you, there is a time for work and a time for rest—it is even said that God rested when the work of creation was finished. To work without rest is to act contrary to the way of the earth. When evening comes it spreads its blanket of darkness over the earth and thus it brings with it sleep. And the seasons too teach us this truth, for while the earth brings forth its fruit in spring, when winter comes even the earth must lay down its bounties. And so it is that I say to you, return to your homes for we too must rest awhile.

Chapter XXXII

Then Drahcira bade her disciples to get into the boat and to go before her to the other side while she sent the people away. And when she had sent them away she went up into a mountain apart to commune with the earth. And when the evening came she was there alone.

2. But the boat was now in the midst of the lake, tossed by the waves. And when the disciples considered that Drahcira would not join them on the other side of the lake, they turned the boat around so that they might return to her.

3. Now as Drahcira made her way down the mountain one of her disciples who was on the boat said that she could swim faster than the ship. And so she dove into the sea and began to swim to the shore. But the distance was greater than she had considered and she grew tired of swimming.

4. And when Drahcira saw how her disciple labored she called out to her saying, "Do not be afraid for I will rescue you!" Then Drahcira dove into the water and swam to her.

5. But when the disciple felt that her strength would give way before Drahcira reached her, she cried out saying, "Teacher, come quickly or I will perish!" And immediately Drahcira stretched forth her hand and caught her.

6. And when the others came with the boat, Drahcira and her disciple entered into it. And Drahcira said to her disciple, "Do not judge the water as evil because you cannot walk upon it (for the

woman cursed the sea) rather see your mistake in judgment—for what you judged to be but a short distance proved to be too great for you—and so it is with all who do not first count the cost of the path they choose."

7. And then speaking to the others she said, "And why is it that you have returned? Did I not tell you that I would join you on the other side? If I told you to go on before me that is what I so intended. Just as I told you that all must rest, so it is that all have need of times of solitude—moments when we can become centered in ourselves and the earth. And thus it was that I stayed behind. But now that we are here in this ship together let us turn around once more and go on to the other side."

8. And when they had passed over they came into a place where Drahcira had spoken and they rested there.

Chapter XXXIII

And it came to pass that the people came again to Drahcira. And they said to her, "What sign can you show us that we may believe your word? The scriptures tell us that the servants of God worked miracles—even giving bread from heaven to our ancestors to eat."

2. Then Drahcira said to them, "Truly I say to you—I work no miracles and the bread that I give is of the earth. And as the earth shares its bread with us, so we must share our bread with others."

3. Then the people complained because she said, "I work no miracles." And they said, "What kind of prophetess is this who works no miracles?"

4. Drahcira therefore said to them, "Do not complain among yourselves. Do you not know that those who ate the 'bread from heaven,' of which you speak of are all now dead? The truth of a prophetess is not measured by the number of 'miracles' she works but rather by the truth of her word—taste and see if my word is not true."

5. Then the people said among themselves, "How can we taste this woman's words? It is rather the bread of heaven that we would taste."

6. Then Drahcira said to them, "Then go taste the 'bread of heaven'—that is, if you can find it, for I cannot give it to you. I speak concerning the earth and not of heaven. Those who would follow me must therefore follow the way of the earth and leave heaven and its bread to the gods!"

7. Two of her disciples, when they heard this said, "This is a hard saying—who can her it?"

8. And when Drahcira knew that two of her disciples were offended by her words she said to them, "Does this offend you? It is the earth that gives life—heaven, at least at the present, remains nothing more than a belief. Have you been with me and heard my teachings and not understood this? The words I speak to you are words of life and the earth. But it seems that you two will not accept the way of the earth."

9. And from that time the two went back and walked with her no more.

Chapter XXXIV

And it came to pass that when Drahcira and her disciples were in a secluded place they took off their clothes to bathe in a certain lake. And when they were done they ate together without putting their clothes back on.

2. And when those who thought themselves holy saw her and her disciples they found fault with them. For those who thought themselves holy never took off their clothes in the presences of another except their spouse."

3. Thus they asked Drahcira, "Why do you and your disciples not walk according to the traditions of our fathers but rather you expose your nakedness in the presence of others?"

4. And she answered and said to them, "You hypocrites, do you believe that our bodies, which even you say God created and declared them 'very good' are evil? No, for it is written, 'I am fearfully and wonderfully made.' Will you contradict the words of scripture and call evil that which they call 'very good' and 'wonderful'? In this you make the words of these scriptures of no effect by your traditions and commandments."

5. Then they answered and said to her, "We do not believe that the body is evil but to look upon the nakedness of another brings evil thoughts of lust."

6. And thus spoke Drahcira: "How is it that if one looks upon the beauties of nature and one's heart is moved with awe, this is considered good? And if one looks upon the sufferings of another

and one's heart is moved with compassion, this is considered good? But if one looks upon the nakedness of another and one's heart is moved with desire, this is considered evil? To be moved with desire when one looks upon the nakedness of another is not evil rather it is the way of the earth. And to act upon this desire is not evil—so long as it is the desire of the other as well. If one is tired, is it evil to desire the pleasure of sleep? If one is hungry, is it evil to desire the pleasure of eating? Then if one desires to share in the pleasure of an other's body, why is this evil?

7. Only desire, which if acted upon would violate an other's freedom of choice can be said to be evil. Truly I say to you, it is impossible not to desire, for even the attempt to overcome desire is itself a desire. Thus it is not desire that is evil but the affect that fulfilling certain desires have upon others. I hold one commandment alone on these matters and it is this, 'Whatever does not violate another person's freedom of choice should be permitted.'"

8. And when Drahcira had finished those who thought themselves holy went their way and from that hour they determined how they might bring her down.

9. And then, turning to her disciples she said, "Hear and understand—the body is not evil but in thinking it can be conceived as such. And thus, for those who think themselves holy to see an other's nakedness arouses desire which they judge to be evil."

10. But her disciples said to her, "Do you not know that they to whom you spoke were offended by you?"

11. But Drahcira said to them, "Let them alone—they are blind leaders of the blind. And our part is to act with true sight lest we fall into the ditch of blindness."

Chapter XXXV

And from there she arose and went to the borderland and entered into a house. And though she didn't want anyone to know that she was there, yet a number of people found her.

2. And there was in that place a young woman who was of a different race than those who had come there. And the people wanted Drahcira to make her go away. For they said, "It is not right to take the children's bread and give it to the dogs!"

3. But the young woman said to them, "Even so, the dogs are allowed to eat the crumbs which fall from their master's table."

4. Then Drahcira said to those who had taken offense in the young woman, "Why is it that you call this woman a dog? Don't you know that the earth has made all people of one blood? Oftentimes I have heard it said that cursing is evil. Cursing however is simply a form of expression regardless of how offensive it may seem to another. But to call those of other races names which demean or insult is a far greater evil for in this you have not taken offense with something that they have said but in who they are as persons—and that they cannot change.

5. "More than this, don't you know that in taking offense at this young woman says more of you than of her, for your attitude reveals fear—fear of that which is different. Haven't you heard that saying of old, 'There is no fear in love for perfect love casts out fear?' And again it is said, 'If a man says I love God and yet hates his brother or sister, he is a liar; for he that doesn't love his brother

or sister whom he has seen, how can he love God whom he has not seen?' Therefore this young woman shall be fed at the same table as you. And if there be any here who takes offense at this, leave now for there is nothing wrong with this woman, rather it is your heart that is wrong."

6. But none would leave for they saw the error in their judgment.

7. And as Drahcira spoke to those who were in that place, many who heard of it came to her, to learn of her and the way of the earth. And as evening drew near, Drahcira ended her teaching but those who came would not leave but slept there in front of the house, waiting for Drahcira to speak again the next day.

8. And on the second day, when she was done speaking to them, she called her disciples and said to them, "I have compassion on these people because they have now been here nearly two days with nothing to eat."

9. And her disciples said to her, "Where can we find enough food to feed so many people?"

10. And Drahcira said, "Go to each house in this town and see what can be found."

11. And when they returned, they gave the food to the people and they were all able to eat. And there were also a number of baskets of food left over.

12. And after this she sent the people away telling them to give the food that was left over to the poor. And Drahcira and her disciples entered the boat and left that town.

Chapter XXXVI

And when her disciples came to the other side they discovered that they had forgotten to bring food. And so when Drahcira said to them, "Beware of the bread of those who think themselves holy"— they said among themselves, "It is because we forgot to bring food."

2. When Drahcira heard this she said to them, "Why do you think like this? For the bread I'm speaking of is the teachings of those who think themselves holy."

3. Then they understood that she was not speaking literally about food, but rather metaphorically of the doctrines of those who think themselves holy.

4. And when they came into the city they met a certain man who could not see that all living things were the children of the earth and thus how even the trees were our kin. And they took the man and led him out of the city among the trees. And after he had learned the way of the earth they returned. And Drahcira asked him what he now saw.

5. And as he looked about he said, "I see trees and they are as valuable as people."

6. And Drahcira sent him away to his house saying, "Into every city and town in which you go be sure to tell this to all."

Chapter XXXVII

And it came to pass when Drahcira was alone with her disciples that she asked them, "Who do people think I am?"

2. And they answered saying, "Some say you are the Messiah or a Buddha or just a dreamer, while others say you are a devil, liar or lunatic."

3. And she asked them, "But who do you say that I am?"

4. And they said, "You are Drahcira, the prophetess of the earth—the voice which speaks on behalf of that which cannot speak."

5. And from that time forth Drahcira began to prepare her disciples for what she saw as inevitable in view of the leaders' attitude towards her and her work—how that some might try to kill her because of her teachings. But she told them that regardless of what might happen they must determine to carry on her work and make it their work.

6. But her disciples took her aside and said, "Be it far from you, Teacher. This shall not happen to you!"

7. But she said to them, "Your words are a disappointment to me for we must think first of the earth or else a time may come when none of our kind shall live."

8. Then she said, "If anyone would follow the way of the earth they must deny their own self-centered interests and think in terms of the whole of the earth. For whoever thinks only of themselves brings hurt to the earth while whoever thinks in terms of the earth

will bring healing to it as well as to themselves. What profit is it if a person gains all that they desire and yet lose the earth? What good is the fulfillment of one's desires if there is no place left to receive them? And once it is no more what can one give in exchange for the earth?"

9. And she took them up into a high mountain and as they communed with the earth it was transfigured before them. And the blue sky and green trees and the brown earth and crystal water shone forth as a living light which is always there and yet is seldom seen.

10. And the disciples said, "It is good for us to be here. Shall we make a temple here to the earth?" And when a cloud came over which overshadowed them, Drahcira said, "See how the sun has hid itself from you? For in your desire to build a temple to the earth you have failed to see that the hour has come when neither on this mountain nor another shall any worship, for the earth itself is our temple—a temple which we have defiled."

11. And when the cloud passed and Drahcira had ended her words, they looked around and saw the earth "As It Is."

12. And her disciples asked her, "Why don't we see the earth transfigured like that more often?"

13. And Drahcira said, "For to see the beauty of the earth and to see the great gift which has been given to us depends not so much on the eyes to see but a heart which appreciates."

Chapter XXXVIII

And when they came down the mountain there was a crowd there. And one of them came to Drahcira and said, "Teacher, please look at my son, my only son—for a demon takes him and suddenly he cries out and foams at the mouth and he falls on the ground and is left bruised."

2. And Drahcira said, "Bring your son here."

3. And as he was coming the boy fell on the ground and began to have seizures and foam at the mouth.

4. And Drahcira asked his father, "How long has your son been troubled by this?"

5. And he said, "Since a child. And often the demon has thrown him into fire or water in order to destroy him. But if you can do anything, have compassion on us and cast out this demon."

6. And Drahcira said to him, "Surely you have heard I am not a healer. I do have compassion on you but I cannot heal your son. But this I will say, that it is *not* a demon which torments your son but a disease, thus take him to a physician and he will do what can be done."

7. And Drahcira took the boy by the hand and lifted him up. And when they went their way she said to the crowd, "You know very well that I am not a healer. I am simply a voice which speaks on behalf of the earth. And though there are many things which I wish were not a part of our world such as pain and suffering, these are a part of it. Our choice therefore in this regard is either

to accept the world 'As It Is' and enjoy what we can, or reject the world and live our lives as if we were prisoners on an evil planet. The message I bring is one of acceptance and those who follow me must see that I offer no escape from the earth but rather a commitment to it."

Chapter XXXIX

And when the crowd left, Drahcira's disciples asked her, "Who is the greatest on the earth?"

2. And at that moment Drahcira saw an earthworm coming up from a muddy place. And she said to them, "Truly I tell you, except you become as this worm you shall not know the way of the earth. For this worm is one with the earth. Neither does it strive to be great—it is what it is and has no need to be seen as better. Truly I tell you, greatness is a human value which we impose on the earth and others. But in truth there are no things greater than any other, for all things have their place in the life of the earth. Humans alone believe that they are the greatest and it is we who endanger the whole, for apart from us the earth lives and moves in perfect harmony."

3. And then one of her disciples said, "Teacher, we saw one who was not of our group teaching as you teach and we didn't like it."

4. But Drahcira said, "Don't dislike this, for if he or she speaks the truth rejoice, for we are not in competition with any who teach the way of the earth, neither do we teach this message in order to be perceived as great. As I said before, in truth there are none greater than any other, though among humans there are teachings which are false and therefore harmful to the earth and to those who dwell therein. Therefore we must rather encourage all who would teach the truth.

5. "But if you had rather told me that you had seen this same man harming a child or a woman, in that case I would have said you were right in disliking him, for whoever would hurt one of these should be turned over to the authorities.

6. Then one of her disciples said, "Teacher, should such a man be forgiven?"

7. And Drahcira said to them, "Of course he should be forgiven, for we understand that anyone who would do such things is troubled himself and needs help and healing. But the fact that we forgive him—understanding why he is the way he is—does not mean that we should not take action to prevent him from repeating such acts. In this we must remember that whatever violates an other's freedom should not be permitted. And though it is true in one sense that in preventing such a person from repeating such acts we are violating their freedom—when one chooses to violate an other's freedom, their freedom must in turn be violated for such acts cannot be permitted."

Chapter XL

Now there was a great holy day coming up so Drahcira's brother said to her, "Go to the festival so that those who come may hear your teachings."

2. But Drahcira said to him, "My time is not yet come. Many hate me because I have spoken against their works and supposed 'truths.'"

3. But after her brother went up to the festival, she went up also but not openly but in secret.

4. And it came to pass that on her way, as she came to a certain town that they would not allow her to enter. And when her disciples saw this they said, "Teacher, should we force our way in?"

5. But she said to them, "You do not realize what you're asking me—for I am not come to force but rather to persuade."

6. And so they continued on until they came to the city where the festival was being held.

7. And many were looking for her saying, "Where is Drahcira?" And there was much talk among the people concerning her. For some said, "She is a good woman" while other said, "No, for she deceives the people."

8. Now in the middle of the festival Drahcira went up to that city's place of worship and taught. And she said, "My doctrine is not a belief or opinion but the truth—and it is not of my own making but of the earth. If any will follow the way of the earth they shall know of the doctrine, whether it be of the earth, or

whether I speak of myself. Those who speak of themselves seek their own glory but those who glory in the earth, the same are true and there is no ill intent in them. Judge not according to appearances but judge in truth."

9. Then some of them said, "Is this not she whom some seek to kill? But she speaks so boldly and they say nothing to her. Do the leaders then know that she is truly the prophetess of the earth?"

10. And many of the people believed her word and said, "When a prophetess comes, will she do more than this woman has done?"

11. And when those who thought themselves holy heard what the people were saying they sent officers to take her away.

12. And Drahcira said to them, "Yet a little while am I with you and then I shall return to the earth from whence I came. You shall not find me—and where I go you cannot follow.

13. Then in the last day, the great day of the festival, Drahcira stood and spoke saying, "If anyone will, let them follow the way of the earth! Those who trust the way of the earth shall live as the water which flows in the rivers."

14. Many of the people, after they had heard Drahcira's teachings said, "Of a truth, she is a prophetess." Others said, "She is the Messiah or a Buddha." But others said, "No, she deceives the people." So there was a division among the people over her. And some of them would have taken her but no one laid hands on her.

15. Then the officers returned to those who had sent them. And they said to the officers, "Why have you not brought her?" And the officers said, "Never has a woman spoken like this." Then those who thought themselves holy said, "Are you also deceived? Have any of the leaders of the people believed her words? Only the people who do not know the scriptures are cursed through her lies!"

16. And everyone went to their own homes but Drahcira departed to a certain mountain to commune with the earth.

Chapter XLI

And early in the morning she came again to the place of worship in that city, and all the people came to her. And she sat down and taught them.

2. And as she taught, those who thought themselves holy laid hold of her and took her to him who was in authority. And when they had set her before him, they said to him, "Master, this woman was teaching in our place of worship. Now the scriptures commands, 'Let your women keep silent in the places of worship, for it is not permitted for them to speak, but they are commanded to be under obedience.' And again it says, 'I do not allow a woman to teach, nor to take authority over man, but to be in silence.' Therefore what should we do?"

3. But Drahcira stooped down and gathered up the dust on the ground in her hands as though she didn't hear them. And when he who was in authority rebuked her, she stood up and said, "Do not your own scriptures say, 'Dust we are and unto dust we shall return?' We are all made of the same dust, thus the words of scripture which these have quoted are in contradiction to the words I have quoted. Male is not greater than female, neither is one grain of dust greater than another."

4. And then Drahcira let the dust fall through her fingers to the ground and they which heard her, being convicted by their own consciences, let her go. And when Drahcira was alone she said to

herself, "I will go and do what I must do and will not be swayed by the condemnation of others."

5. But after Drahcira left, those who thought themselves holy were sorry that they let her go and steadfastly determined to lay hold of her again.

Chapter XLII

Then Drahcira spoke to them again saying, "I am a voice for the earth—whoever hears my voice and follows me shall walk in the way of the earth."

2. Some there therefore said to her, "That is your opinion and your opinion is not true!"

3. But Drahcira answered them saying, "Is it not written in your scriptures that you must 'Prove all things and hold fast to that which is good?' How have you proven my words to be untrue? This you have not done, rather you have simply rejected my words because they do not agree with your beliefs. You judge all by your scriptures which themselves cannot be proven to be true. I judge in terms of the way of the earth whose way is here for all to see."

4. Then Drahcira said, "I go my way and soon you will seek me but where I go you cannot follow." Then they said, "Will you kill yourself?—for you said, 'Where I go you cannot follow.'"

5. Then she said to them, "We are all of the flesh—and flesh is but dust. Do you know that we shall all one day return to the earth from whence we came?—and in this all must make their journey alone."

6. And as she spoke to them there were many who understood her. But when Drahcira said, "If you continue in my word then you are indeed my disciples and you shall know the truth and the truth shall set you free," some answered and said to her, "We are not in bondage to anyone—so how can you say that you will set us free?"

7. And Drahcira said to them, "I must answer you on two points. First, you must understand that I did not say that *'I'* would set you free but the *truth* would set you free. Secondly, whenever one lives in opposition to the way of the earth, one is not free to be what one truly is. Truly I say to you, the hour is coming and now is when we must bring our lives into harmony with the way of the earth or else the earth as we have known it will pass away—thus it is that I have said that the truth shall set you free—for you are not yet truly free."

8. Then they answered her saying, "God is our Father and we are already free in Him."

9. But Drahcira said to them, "If you were God's children, you would do the works of God. But now there are some who seek to kill me—a woman who has only told you the truth—this does not seem to be in accord with a God whom your own scriptures say is 'Love.' You do rather the deeds of your father whose name is 'Fear.'"

10. Then they said to her, "We were not born of fornication as you were. We have one Father who is God. You don't even know who your real father was."

11. Drahcira therefore said to them, "If God were your Father, you would love me, for your scriptures say, 'If a man says I love God and hates his brother, he is a liar, for he who does not love his brother whom he has seen, how can he love God whom he has not seen?'"

12. And with these words Drahcira left and went to another town.

Chapter XLIII

And she came upon a certain lawyer who asked her, "Teacher, what must I do to be assured of eternal life?" And Drahcira said to him, "What is written in your scriptures? What do you understand them to say?"

2. And he answered her saying, "I must love the Lord my God with all my heart and with all my soul and with all my strength and with all of my mind—and my neighbor as myself."

3. And Drahcira said to him, "You have answered well. But I would say a few things to you. Though your question concerns 'eternal life,' I do not know what lies beyond the grave—maybe there is another life but I don't know with any certainty. All I know is the life we live here and now. But I do know this, that if you would love the world to the same degree that your scriptures say you must love God, you would not need to worry about eternal life for the life you live here would become so rich and fulfilling that you would long for nothing more."

4. But the lawyer, in an attempt to avoid Drahcira's word asked her, "And what about loving my neighbor as myself?"

5. And thus spoke Drahcira: "In truth we do all love our neighbors as ourselves. The problem however is the degree we love ourselves. That is, because many love themselves so little they also love others little.

6. "Now there was a certain man, the husband of a wife he had married when they were young. As the years went by his wife

bore him children and served him with such devotion that she did not follow her own dreams. Then one day the man's wife came to herself and determined to leave her husband so that she might fulfill her own dreams rather than his alone. But the man would not hear of it and swore that his love for her was so great that if she left him he would kill himself, for he couldn't live without her. And so his wife, not willing to bear the burden of his death gave up her dreams and returned to her husband and lived out her life as he so determined.

7. "Now, which of these did truly love themselves?—the husband or the wife?" And the lawyer said, "Neither." And Drahcira said, "In this you have spoken the truth, for if the husband thought he would die if his wife chose to follow her own path, this would show that not only did he not love himself (in that he would kill himself) but that he did not really love his wife or else he would have allowed her to fulfill her dreams. And if the wife would give up following her dreams in order to prevent her husband's death, this would show that she did not truly love herself (in that she would leave her dreams unfulfilled). And though it might be perceived as if her choice to forsake her path was an act of love, in truth it would be an act of fear—the fear of letting her husband do what she would not have him do as well as the fear of being judged as the cause of his death. In all of this, what is said to be love is rather dependence and a fear to be oneself."

8. And with this Drahcira left that place.

Chapter XLIV

And as Drahcira passed by she saw a man who was blind from birth. And her disciples asked her, "Teacher, who sinned that this man was born blind?—he or his parents?"

2. And Drahcira answered, "First, if it was this man, you would have to assume that he had sinned in a past life in order to be born blind in this life. But in truth blindness is not the result of sin. Such a belief comes from the teachings of those who think themselves holy—and you should not hold such views.

3. After she had said this she spit on the ground and said, "Thus I spit out of my mouth all such beliefs." And after saying goodbye to the blind man they went on.

4. But when the neighbors of the blind man knew that he had been with Drahcira and saw that he was not better, they brought those who thought themselves holy to show Drahcira could not work miracles but rather that she only spit out words and thus she was surely no prophetess.

5. And so those who thought themselves holy asked the man what Drahcira had done. And he said to them, "After saying that my blindness was not caused by sin, she spit on the ground and said, "Thus I spit out of my mouth all such beliefs."

6. And they said to him, "Surely this woman cannot be a prophetess for she does no miracles—she is rather a sinner!"

7. Therefore the blind man said, "Whether she is a sinner or not I do not know. One thing I do know and that is I am still blind."

8. And it came to pass that later that day Drahcira came upon the blind man again. And when she saw him she said to him, "Do you believe in the way of the earth?" And the blind man said, "No, for the way of the earth is the way of 'The Fall,' sin and blindness—and no good can come out of it."

9. And Drahcira said to him, "You are far more blind that you know, for even if I could have given you your sight you still would have remained blind to the truth of the way of the earth."

10. And with these words she left the man.

Chapter XLV

And when it was the time of the great winter festival, Drahcira walked into the most prominent place of worship, and when a crowd gathered they said to her, ""How long will you keep us uncertain? If you are a prophetess of God, tell us plainly."

2. And Drahcira answered them saying, "I have told you but you do not hear. The works that I do are for the earth and not for God!"

3. Then they took up stones to stone her. But Drahcira said to them, "I have done no one harm, why then will you stone me?" And they answered, "You may not have harmed anyone's body but your teachings are killing the spirits of those who had once set themselves apart for God and the world-to-come!"

4. And Drahcira said to them, "And you will right my supposed wrong by killing me? Is your truth such that the only way it can be defended is by killing those who do not agree with it?"

5. And as the crowd argued among themselves concerning Drahcira's words, she escaped out of their hands.

Chapter XLVI

Now there was a certain man whom Drahcira loved more than any other. And when it was found that he was sick, word was sent to her saying, "Teacher, he whom you love is very sick."

2. Now when Drahcira heard this she did not consider it to be a sickness that would end in death. And so she stayed where she was for two more days. But when the two days were past she said to her disciples, "We must go back, for I must see that all is well with him."

3. But her disciples said to her, "Teacher, the people in the town where he lives are determined to stone you—so why do you want to go back there?"

4. Drahcira answered, "Are there not twelve hours in a day? As we must work while it is day, so we must share our love with our friends while they yet have days to share. Now I am truly sorry that I did not leave immediately upon hearing of his sickness."

5. Then one of the disciples said to the others, "Let us go so we can die with her."

6. And when Drahcira came to that town she found that he had died the day before they came.

7. At the man's house there were many there who had come to comfort the man's family, and when they heard that Drahcira had come they met her and said to her that if she had been here he might not have died.

8. Drahcira however said nothing. But when she saw the man whom she loved above all others lying there forever beyond her reach, she fell down before him and wept.

9. Then some who were there said, "She must have loved him very much!" But others there said, "If she had been here couldn't she have saved him?"

10. Then as they carried his body to the grave, Drahcira followed and groaned in anguish at her loss.

11. And before they laid him in the grave she kissed him once more. And once he was buried, though Drahcira was crying she said, "We must let him go for he has now returned to the earth who gave him to us. And though we may regret not having been all we could have for him—as I most surely do—we cannot go back and do what we would do now. It is finished. But though he is dead he will continue to live in our memories but never enough to satisfy the longing of my heart. Oh, to make love to him just once more— but then again, once more would never be enough. And thus we must live with this pain even as the land's edge must live with the river which wears it away. Hail and farewell my love."

12. And when Drahcira left, her disciples followed and all wondered whether Drahcira would yet love the earth which had taken her love and whether she would again teach the gospel of the way of the earth.

Chapter XLVII

One day quite a few unbelievers came to her and those who thought themselves holy complained saying, "This woman receives sinners and even socializes with them."

2. And so Drahcira told them this parable: "Who of you, having two or three children, if one was lost would not leave the others in order to find the one who was lost? And when you found the child, would you not come home rejoicing, saying to your neighbors, 'Rejoice with me for I have found my child who was lost?' I tell you that likewise I rejoice in receiving these whom you judge to be 'lost sinners.'"

3. And she also said, "A certain man had two sons. And the younger son said to his father, 'Father, give me my portion of our inheritance.' And so he divided the inheritance between them. A few days later the younger son gathered his things together and left home for a city far away. But there he wasted away his fortune on wine, women and song. And when he had spent all that he had, he had to try to find a job to support himself. But all he could find was a job as a dishwasher. But one day he came to himself and said, 'My father's workers have good jobs, homes and plenty to eat. I'm going to go back home and tell my father that I have made a terrible mistake and am no longer worthy to be called his son. I will be satisfied if he but takes me on as one of his workers.

4. "And so he arose and went to his father. But as he neared his home, though he was yet a great way off, his father saw him and

in love ran to him and embraced him. And the son said to him, 'Father, I have made a terrible mistake and am no longer worthy to be called your son!' But his father said, 'Son, all people make mistakes. It is true that some seem to be greater than others but we all do things which we later regret. The most important thing is that we learn from our mistakes, continue to love others despite their wrongs and never consider another to be lost—that is to be beyond hope. Only those who think themselves holy can in their ignorance judge those unlike themselves as lost—even when their own scriptures tell them to 'Judge not lest you be judged.' And so it was that the father made a great feast and said to all who came, 'Let us eat, drink and be merry, for this is my son who thought himself lost but who has found this day that love sees what eyes cannot see.'"

Chapter XLVIII

And Drahcira said to her disciples, "The children of this world are in their generation wiser than 'the children of light.'"

2. But when those who thought themselves holy heard this they mocked her.

3. Drahcira said to them, "You are they who justify yourselves before God but we know your hearts, for that which you claim is highly esteemed of God is an abomination to those who follow the way of the earth. The gospel of the kingdom of heaven is said to have been preached until now—hereafter the gospel of the way of the earth shall be preached—and even now there are many who are ready to hear it.

4. "According to your 'Word of God' it is said that there was a certain rich man who was dressed in fine clothes and had great riches. And then there was a beggar who was full of sores who lay at the rich man's gates, hoping to be fed by the scraps that were left from the rich man's table. And it came to pass that the beggar died and was carried by angels to heaven. And then in time the rich man died and was buried—and in hell he lifted up his eyes, being in torment and saw the beggar afar off in heaven. And he cried to the beggar, 'Have mercy on me and dip your finger in water and cool my tongue for I am tormented in these flames.' But the beggar said, 'Remember that in your lifetime you received good things while I only bad—but now I am comforted while you are tormented. And besides this, there is a great gulf fixed between us so that they who

would pass from here to you cannot—neither can you pass to us. Then the rich man said, 'I pray then that you would send someone to my father's house, for I have five brothers. Warn them lest they too come into this place of torment.' And the beggar said, 'They have the word of God—let them hear It!' And he said, 'No, for if one went to them from the dead they would believe and repent.' But the beggar said, 'If they will not hear the word of God they will not believe even if one rose from the dead.'

5. "Though one of the intents of this passage of scripture is good—for it shows the injustices of the rich who disregard the need of the poor and homeless—feeling no responsibility to those beyond their own gates. Two of its other intents are not good in terms of the way of the earth. First, it suggests that justice is met out in the world-to-come, which is beyond our knowing, rather than focusing on the need for justice in the world-here-and-now. Second, in its closing lines it makes the 'word of God' the basis for motivating people to act just. The problem is that there are many 'words of God' which hold forth standards of justice—sometimes completely at odds with each other and thus their authority is arbitrary. Therefore I say to you that the basis of justice is not a matter of the authority of any scripture but rather a matter of compassion and a recognition of the interdependence of all things in our world."

6. And her disciples said to her, "Teacher, increase our faith in the way of the earth."

7. And she said, "If you have but the faith of a grain of mustard seed, you have what is needed, for just as the mustard seed does not stay small but grows into a plant which brings both spice and healing, so shall your faith in the way of the earth grow, bringing with it both healing and spice to your lives."

Chapter XLIX

And again, those who thought themselves holy came to Drahcira and asked her, "Is it true that whoever divorces his wife and marries another commits adultery against her?"

2. And Drahcira answered them, saying, "There is no law of nature which requires one to be bound to another so long as they live. And most of the laws which are claimed to be the laws of God are in truth but the traditions of men—who have seen women as their possessions.

3. "In the way of the earth some animals mate for life while others do not and both are acting according to their natures. We however do not have fixed natures in this regard, for there are some who desire to be bound to only one for their lifetime, while there are others who desire to be bound to another for only a time, while there are still others who would rather not be bound to any. Nature has not made us all the same and therefore it is against nature and thus against the way of the earth to make laws which would demand that all be the same in this regard."

4. And those who thought themselves holy said, "And what of those who desire to have relations with those of their same sex? Not only is this against the law of God, is it not also against the law of nature and what you call 'the way of the earth?'"

5. And Drahcira answered them saying, "Strange as it may seem to you, those who desire to have relations with those of their same sex are also acting according to the way of the earth for these

people are found among every nation, kindred and tongue—nearly ten percent of every people—that is a tithe. And they don't choose this it is who they are by nature. More than this, same sex behavior has been observed in well over a thousand species. So no, it is not against the law of nature and in this your law of God is untrue."

6. And with this those who thought themselves holy left with great wrath against Drahcira and her teachings.

Chapter L

Then were there brought to Drahcira little children, so that she would lay her hands upon them and bless them. But she said, "How can I bless those who are already blessed, for such are of the earth. To think that these are born in sin or must be blessed to be holy is to err in your thoughts for these children have come into the world in purity and through that act which is the way of the earth."

2. And when she had said this there came one running who knelt before her and asked, "Teacher, what shall I do that I may inherit the earth?" And Drahcira said to him, "Why do you call be good as if you are not? All are good, apart from the fears which move them to hurt others as well as themselves. The earth need not be inherited for it is already yours. But if you would know what you should do, I say to you, 'And it harm none, do what you will.'"

3. And when the man heard this he rejoiced for now he saw the earth and the fullness thereof as his own.

4. And Drahcira looked around her and said to her disciples, "How beautiful is the way of the earth. Truly I say to you, as easy as it is for a camel to walk when fully refreshed, so should it be for those who walk in the way of the earth."

5. And they were amazed saying, "Who then should not walk in this way?" And Drahcira, looking upon them said, "All those who believe it impossible."

6. Then one of her disciples said to her, "We have left all to follow the way of the earth."

7. But Drahcira said, "Truly I say to you, how can you leave all in following the way of the earth when all is on the earth. In truth all one needs to leave is a certain way of thinking which sees the earth as either an object to be possessed and plundered or a mistake to be overcome when one goes to heaven."

8. And when some complained concerning the fact that the earth gave some its bounties while others very little, Drahcira said, "The earth is like a man who went out early in the morning to hire laborers for his vineyard. And when he had agreed with the laborers for a certain amount a day he sent them out into his vineyard. And then he went out later and saw others standing idle in the market place and said to them, 'Go into my vineyard and I will give you wages.' And they went their way. Then later he went out and did the same thing with other laborers. Then finally near the end of the day he found others standing idle and said to them, 'Why stand here idle?' And they said to him, 'because no one has hired us.' And so he said to them, 'You go also into my vineyard and I will give you wages.' So when the evening came the owner of the vineyard called the laborers in beginning from the last unto the first. And when those who were hired first saw that the owner paid those who had come last the same, they complained to the owner saying, 'These last have worked only one hour and you have paid them equal to us who have borne the burden and heat of the day!' But he answered them and said, 'Friends, I have done you no wrong. Did you not receive what you agreed to work for? Take it and go your way. Can't I do with my money as I please? Is what I have given you unworthy of your appreciation because I have been more generous with others in terms of their work?' Therefore, neither should the earth be considered evil in that it does not give of its bounties in the way you believe it should."

Chapter LI

Then Drahcira took her disciples and said to them, "We will now go up to the 'holy city' even though I may be handed over to the leaders of the people."

2. And while she yet spoke the mother of two of her disciples came to her, desiring a certain thing of her. And she said to her, "What is it you want?"

3. And she said, "Grant that my son and daughter may sit on your right and your left hand in your kingdom."

4. But Drahcira answered her saying, "You do not know what you are asking. I am not a king or queen nor do I have a kingdom. I am only a voice crying in the wilderness—'Prepare the way of the earth!' More than this, though the kings of this earth exercise dominion over others—choosing who shall sit in each place of authority, it is not so among us. Rather those who are great among us act as the servants of those who are less fortunate."

5. And as they went their way there was a rich man who wanted to see Drahcira but could not because of the crowd, for he was small of stature. So the man ran ahead of the crowd and climbed up into a sycamore tree to see her, for Drahcira was going to pass that way.

6. And when Drahcira came to that place she looked up and saw the man in the tree and said, "Come down for today I will come to your house." And the man got down quickly and received her into his house joyfully.

7. And when the crowd saw this they complained saying that she has gone to be the guest of a man who is a "sinner."

8. And the man said to Drahcira, "Teacher, half of all I have I will give to support the gospel of the way of the earth and if I have gained any of my wealth through fraud I will restore it fourfold."

9. Therefore Drahcira said to him, "This day you have caused the earth to rejoice!"

10. And when she had said this they ate together and then she went her way towards the "holy city" with her disciples.

11. And a great holy day was near and many came from all over the country to the "holy city" before the holy day to purify themselves. And the people looked for Drahcira and spoke among themselves as they stood in the place of worship saying, "What do you think? Will she come to the feast?"

12. Now the leaders of the people had given command that if anyone knew where Drahcira was they should report it so that she might be taken.

Chapter LII

And it came to pass when she was near to the "holy city"—at the mount before it, she sent four of her disciples saying, "Go into the village which is before the 'holy city' and find four horses: one white, one red, one black and the other brown. The white horses shall carry two cages of doves, the red horse shall carry incense, the black horse shall carry two buckets of water, and the brown horse shall carry dirt in its saddle bags. And if anyone asks you why you are gathering these things, you shall say to them, 'Because Drahcira is preparing a procession to honor the earth. After the procession is complete we shall return to you your horses and these things.'"

2. And as they were gathering all that Drahcira had said, they were asked why they were gathering these things and they said what Drahcira had told them to say.

3. And then later they brought the horses laden with the things Drahcira had requested. And they began to walk in procession around the "holy city" and many men, women and children joined them in their procession to honor the earth.

4. And when they came to the east of the city they paused and Drahcira opened the cages filled with doves which the white horse bore and all but one dove flew away. Therefore Drahcira reached into the cage and took the dove in her hands and casting it up into the sky said, "We call upon you to be our witness O Father Sky. How can we ever thank you enough, for you have breathed into our nostrils the breath of life and thus we live. You share yourself

with all without price—Blessed be!" And having said this they continued their procession around the circle of the city.

5. And when they came to the south of the city they paused and Drahcira waved the incense which the red horse carried unto the sun and said, "We call upon you to be our witness O sun, moon and stars. We thank you for shining your light upon us— you share yourselves with all without price—Blessed be!" And having said this they again continued in their procession around the circle of the city.

6. And when they came to the west of the city they again paused and Drahcira cupped her hands and drew water from the buckets on the black horse and she poured it upon the earth saying, "We call upon you waters of the earth and all that live therein to be our witnesses. We are thankful for the waters which cleanse, refresh and give life. You are here for all without price—Blessed be!" And having said they continued in their procession around the circle of the city.

7. And when they came to the north of the city they paused once more and Drahcira asked for two of the children to come to her. And she had them each reach into the saddle bags and bring out a handful of dirt. And she told them to sprinkle the dirt on the ground and as they did she said, "We call upon you to be our witness O Mother Earth. How can we ever thank you enough, for we are bone of your bones and flesh of your flesh, in that we are dust. And this dirt which is of the earth, sustains us with its bounty of crops, vineyards, and beautiful flowers and trees which delight our eyes. You are here for all without price—Blessed be!" And having said this she knelt down and kissed the earth.

8. Then returning to the east of the city Drahcira said, "Give us wisdom that what we do within this circle will be for the good of the earth and for all who dwell therein. So mote it be and blessed be!"

9. And having said this, Drahcira led the procession into the city on the brown horse while three of the disciples that had borrowed the horses followed her. And as they proceeded those who

were with her followed and others joined the procession shouting, "Blessed is she who teaches the gospel of the way of the earth!"

10. And those who thought themselves holy said among themselves, "It seems like we are doing nothing to stop her, for the people are following her!" And therefore some of them told Drahcira to tell the people be quiet. But she said to them, "I tell you that if these would hold their peace, the very earth would cry out!"

11. And as she was in the city she wept and said to those who thought themselves holy, "If only you could see the things that have been given you—but you are blind. For if you do not heed the gospel of the way of the earth, the days shall come when your children shall be as dung upon the earth because you did not know the time of your visitation."

12. And when it was evening Drahcira and her disciples made their beds upon the earth within the "holy city."

Chapter LIII

Now in the morning when Drahcira awoke she was hungry. And when she saw a fig tree in the way, she came up to it, and plucking its fruit she gave it to her disciples and they ate of it—giving thanks to the earth. And having eaten they went on their way.

2. And at length they came to the place of worship in that city. And on that same day those who had come were selling certain goods in order to make profit for the place of worship. And when Drahcira saw those who bought and sold, she passed by their tables. And she said to them all, "So this is your 'house of prayer?' I would make my house elsewhere—among the rocks and trees and streams of water. Truly I say to you that the earth was given to us as a house of prayer for all nations. But you have made it, as you have made this place—a den of thieves."

3. And those who thought themselves holy sought how they might bring her down but they feared her for the people were amazed by what she taught and the way she taught it.

4. And when they asked her by what authority did she teach such things, she answered them saying, "I will also ask you one thing, which if you answer me, I will likewise tell you by what authority I teach these things. Is the way of the earth of God or of man?"

5. And they discussed this among themselves saying, "If we say of God she will say to us 'Then why do you not accept this

message?' But if we say of men we fear that the people will consider us to be fools for all hold that God created the earth."

6. And thus they answered Drahcira saying, "We do not know." Therefore she said to them, "Then neither will I tell you by what authority I teach these things."

7. And turning to the people she said, "Have you ever read in the scriptures, 'The stone which the builders rejected, the same has become the corner stone?' Truly I say to you, this world is the stone which the builders of this place of worship have rejected and it is the cornerstone—that is to say, it is the foundation of our life. And those who reject it, have during their lives, sought to grind it to powder. Yet, when they fall upon it, the earth shall receive them into her bosom and embrace them regardless of what they have done to her.

8. And when those who thought themselves holy heard these things, they thought that she was speaking of them. But none sought to lay hold of her for they feared the people, because they took her to be a prophetess.

Chapter LIV

Then those who thought themselves holy went and took counsel concerning how they might entangle her, in what she taught.

2. And they sent out to her some of their own along with a certain tax collector who said, "Teacher, we know that you are true and teach the way of the earth in truth, neither do you care for any more than another regardless of their position. Therefore tell us, what do you think? Does the earth belong freely to us all or must we pay property tax to those in authority, for its use?"

3. But Drahcira sensed their intent and thus said to them, "Why do you tempt me you hypocrites? Look at the earth. Whose name does it bear? It belongs to none. Rather it is a gift to us all. And yet men in their ignorance have thought that the earth could be possessed—bought, sold and taxed. More than this, once possessed they have arrogantly believed that it was theirs to do with whatever they pleased. Truly I say to you, we have become to the earth as cancer is to the body!"

4. So they said to her, "Therefore, what is your answer? Must we pay property tax or not?"

5. And Drahcira said to them, "Render unto those in authority those things which are theirs. And let us cease rendering hurt to the earth."

6. And on that same day their came to her those of a certain group which did not believe in the doctrine of the resurrection at the "Last Day," and they asked her, "If a married man dies and

another takes his wife and marries her, who of these shall be her husband in the resurrection?"

7. And Drahcira answered them saying, I as you, do not believe in the resurrection of the dead. Therefore I would say neither. In the scripture it is said that a man leaves his father and mother and is joined to his wife and they being two become one flesh. I however say that once one dies his body is joined to the earth and the flesh of his body becomes one with the dust of the earth. But who can know for certain what becomes of the spirit of those who die. On this matter I speak neither yea nor nay."

8. And when they heard her answer they were amazed that one esteemed as a prophetess would think as they on this matter.

9. But when those who thought themselves holy heard these things, one of them who was a lawyer asked her, "Teacher, which is the greatest commandment of the law?"

10. And Drahcira answered saying, "I live by but one law and it is this, 'Whatever does not violate another person's freedom of choice should be permitted' or as the ancients once said, 'And it harm none, do what you will.' And if you would know anything more, I would simply say that these words of the ancients must be observed not only with regard to how one person treats another but with regard to how one treats the earth and the fullness thereof."

Chapter LV

Then Drahcira spoke to the crowd and to her disciples saying, "Many of the religious leaders bind heavy burdens, which are hard to bear upon the shoulders of those who trust them—and they will not even lift a finger to help them. And all of their works they do to be seen of others. They love to wear long robes and sit in places of high regard. Furthermore, they love to be addressed by titles of honor. And speaking to the religious leaders she said:

2. "Woe to you who love to make long prayers, hoping to be admired by others, for when your arrogance is seen for what it is your humiliation will be seven-fold.

"And woe to you who decide who shall enter the kingdom of heaven and who shall rather go to hell, for the life you say must be lived in order to enter the kingdom of heaven has in truth made this life a hell.

"And woe to you who compass the word to make one convert, for when he is made, he is twice the child of hell than you are yourselves.

"And woe to you who devour the purses of those who trust you, for one day the earth shall devour your flesh.

"And woe to you who make yourselves outwardly clean, while within you are full of all uncleanness and hypocrisy.

"And woe to you who garnish the tombs of the prophets, saying that if you had lived in days past you would not have been guilty of their blood—while secretly you seek my blood."

3. And when she had finished these words, the religious leaders were furious. But when she looked up she saw rich men casting their gifts into the treasury of the place of worship upon the grounds where she spoke. And then she saw a certain poor widow who cast in just two coins.

4. And she said, "Of a truth, I say to you that this poor widow has cast in more than all of them, for the others have from their abundance given to the treasury, but she being poor has given all that she has. And though for this she is rich in spirit more than they, yet she has been robbed on account of the beliefs of those who think themselves holy and who teach that to live is to support their cause and to die is gain. Woe be to them!"

5. And many believed Drahcira's words—even some among the religious leaders, though they would not confess this, lest they be put out of the place of worship.

6. Therefore Drahcira cried out saying, "Those who believe in me, believe not in me but the earth, for I am but a voice crying in the wilderness saying, 'Prepare the way of the earth!'"

7. And with this Drahcira departed from the place of worship.

Chapter LVI

And as they sat down in a certain place not far from the place of worship, her disciples asked her, "Tell us what will be the signs of 'the end of the world?'"

2. And Drahcira answered them saying, "Be careful that you are not deceived by those claiming to prophesy the message of God. For they want the world to come to an end, so that they may be in 'the-world-to-come.' They will say that wars, famines, pestilence and earthquakes are signs that the end is near, even at the door.

3. "But of this they are willingly ignorant for they are not prophesying the will of God in this but rather they are projecting their own will upon the world.

4. "Of a truth, from the dawn of our race there have been famines, pestilences and earthquakes—and there have been wars as well. And though prophets have declared these to be signs of the end of the world in every generation, their words ring true in this generation for we too have seen these things.

5. "The earth has always brought things to our doors which most have seen as evil—that is, famines, pestilence, earthquake and the like. But now, our race, through selfishness, has added evil unto evil, for we have not only raped and plundered the earth but we have made it altogether an unclean thing.

6. "More than this, where once wars threatened tribe and nation, now they threaten the whole earth, and none, not even the innocent shall escape its ravages.

7. "Therefore, this gospel of the way of the earth must be taught in all the world for a witness to all nations and then shall the end be averted."

8. And when Drahcira finished saying these things she told them this parable: "Behold the fig tree. When its leaves fall from its branches as dead upon the ground, you know that winter is near. So likewise when you see all these things know that the end of the world as we know it is near, even at the door.

9. "But know this as well: Though when winter comes we cannot turn back the wheel of the year, yet we can avert the end which knocks upon our door—but this only by walking in the way of the earth. If we do not, the wheel will turn and crush us in its way. Life will arise again, as spring follows winter but it may arise without us."

Chapter LVII

And after two days the great feast was to begin and the religious leaders met to plan how they might destroy Drahcira, but some said, "Not on the feast day for there may be an uproar among the people."

2. Now, as Drahcira was the guest of a certain woman in that city, and as she sat to eat, there came a man having an alabaster bottle of very precious oil.

3. And coming before Drahcira, he asked her to stand. And when she had he told her to stand in the form of a star—with arms and legs outstretched.

4. And when she had done so, he knelt down before her, and anointed her feet with oil he saying, "How beautiful are the feet of one who teaches the gospel of the way of the earth and who brings glad tidings of joy!"

5. Then rising, he anointed each of her hands saying, "Whatever your hands must do, do it with all of your might, for there is neither work nor thought in the grave, where we all must go!"

6. Then touching her forehead with the oil he said, "I bless this which has seen what few eyes have seen and what few ears have heard—knowledge too wonderful for those whose hope is in 'the-world-to-come!'"

7. And with this he kissed her upon the lips which had spoken the truth to all saying, "I have consecrated you that you may do what must be done within the circle of this city."

8. And there were some there who were filled with anger who said, "Why has this man done this?" And they complained about the man.

9. And Drahcira said, "Let him alone. Why do you trouble him? He has done a good thing for me. For in anointing me he has consecrated me for what remains of the works I must do. And truly I say to you, 'Wherever the gospel of the way of the earth is taught, may what this man has done tonight be remembered.'"

Chapter LVIII

Now on the first day of the feast the disciples came to Drahcira and asked her, "Where will we eat tonight?"

2. And she told them to go to a certain man and say to him that Drahcira would like to share the feast at his house.

3. And when they found the man he showed them a large upper room furnished and prepared.

4. Now when evening came Drahcira sat down with her disciples. And seeing they were all there and sensing that her time was short she said to them, "You call me 'Teacher' and in this you are right, for so I am. But in truth, the earth itself is our greatest teacher. Have you not read, 'Ask the animals and they shall teach you and the birds of the air and they shall tell you—or speak to the earth and it shall teach you and the fish of the sea shall declare unto you. Day unto day utters speech and night unto night shows knowledge. There is no speech or language—and yet without these their voices are heard. Their line has gone out through all the earth and their words to the end of the world.' And more than this everyone is to you a teacher and you in turn are yourselves teachers to all. Learn your lessens well for I shall not always be with you."

5. And as they were eating Drahcira took a loaf of bread and giving it to her disciples she said, "Eat this for it is a child born from the union of our kind with the earth. For its substance came forth from the womb of the earth and yet we gave it its form."

6. And then taking a bottle of wine she gave it to them saying, "Drink this always remembering where it came from. For these grapes too were taken from the earth and crushed that their blood might fill our cups. And though wine makes our hearts glad, yet we must remember to drink it in moderation.

7. "Let not your hearts be troubled. You believe in me—believe even more in the way of the earth. In our Mother's house there is room enough for all but all must be true to her ways. I have taught the way of the earth and I encourage you to do the same."

8. Then one of her disciples asked, "Teacher, show us the 'Mother' and then we will be satisfied."

9. And Drahcira said to him, "Have I been with you so long and you do not know that our 'Mother' is the earth? We were born of her womb and suckled at her breasts. And we live out our days upon her body and in death we are buried within her womb from whence we came.

10. "In peace we meet, in peace we now part. Blessed be!"

Chapter LIX

Later that evening as they went their way, Drahcira said to her disciples, "The earth is the vine and we are the branches. Every branch which abides in the vine, the same brings much fruit but if the branch does not abide in the vine, it withers and is cast into the fire and is burned.

2. "These things I say to you that you remember your debt to the earth, for there shall come a time that whoever shall kill us will think they do God a favor. And these things they will do to you because they have not known the way of the earth, or me.

3. "I have yet many things to say to you but you are not ready to hear them now. But if you have ears to hear, the earth will teach you everything you need to know.

4. "We have now entered the times of birth pangs. A woman when she is experiencing her birth pangs is fearful because her hour has come and she is unsure of the outcome, but as soon as she is delivered of her child, she is relieved and remembers her pains no more. Likewise our cause too is in a time of birth pangs but remember that just as when a woman's birth pains are past she remembers them no more but rejoices, so we too must look to the days of rejoicing when all shall follow the way of the earth. But woe to the earth if this gospel is aborted! For eye has not seen nor ear heard—neither has entered into our hearts those things which will come upon us."

5. And when they came to a certain hill, Drahcira said to her disciples, "Sit here while I go and contemplate what lies ahead."

6. And when she had gone just a short way away she felt great grief, and she said to them, "My soul is grieving, even to the point of death."

7. And she went a little further and fell on the ground and said, "O Mother, I fear that the religious leaders will soon vent their anger upon me—one who has sought only to speak on your behalf. I must not fall into the temptation to turn aside from the path that I have set before myself—may my spirit be as strong as my flesh for that which is yet to come!"

Chapter LX

And while she was speaking a number of soldiers who were sent by the religious leaders came with weapons.

2. Therefore Drahcira asked them, "Who do you seek?" And they answered, "Drahcira." And Drahcira said, "I am she. Take me but let those who are with me go."

3. And so they led Drahcira away to the religious leaders and left her disciples behind.

4. And when she appeared before the council they questioned her concerning her doctrine. But Drahcira answered them saying, "I have spoken openly and there is nothing that I have taught in secret. Why do you ask me? Some of your own have heard what I have taught—they know what I have said."

5. And when she had said this one of the officers which stood by slapped Drahcira saying, "This is not how you should speak to the council!"

6. And Drahcira said to him, "If I have spoken disrespectful I might understand why you slapped me but I have said nothing disrespectful." And then to the council she said, "And what are the charges against me? What have I done wrong?"

7. And then came in two witnesses who said, "She is a witch for we saw her cast a circle about our city and she practices such things which are of the devil which shall bring evil upon us and our children!"

8. And the council rose and said to her, "What do you say for yourself?"

9. And Drahcira said to them, "It is not I who seek to bring evil upon you and your children, rather it is you who through your selfish rape and plunder of the earth are bringing evil upon us all. Furthermore, what you call 'practicing things of the devil' are rather my ways of showing reverence to the earth."

10. Then they said to her, "By Almighty God we demand that you tell us whether you are a witch or not!" But Drahcira held her peace and said nothing. And again they asked her demanding an answer, and this time Drahcira said, "I am but a voice which speaks on behalf of the earth!"

11. But at this the council said, "Your refusal to answer our question has proved your undoing, for we have no further need of witnesses—for your silence has condemned you!"

12. Then he that led the council said to them, "The scriptures say that 'Thou shalt not allow a witch to live.' What is your decision?" And they answered and said, "She is worthy of death!" And some spit on her.

13. And in the morning they took her and turned her over to the governor. And they began to accuse her saying, "We found this woman worthy of death!"

14. And because it was not lawful to put anyone to death on religious grounds they said that she was guilty of sedition.

15. Therefore the governor questioned Drahcira saying, "Is it true that you seek to overthrow the present order?" And Drahcira said, "I only teach that our loyalty must be first to the earth. Therefore whatever any government does which brings hurt to the earth and its ways must be stopped! Furthermore, anyone who would know the truth will hear the voice of the earth."

16. And the governor answered her and said, "What is truth?" And when he had said this he went out to the religious leaders and said to them, "I do not find this woman worthy of death."

17. But they were even more insistent saying, "She is stirring up the people, teaching her lies throughout the whole region!"

18. And the governor answered and said to them, "What shall I do with her who is called, Drahcira?" And they said, "Burn her!" But he said, "Why, what evil has she done?" But they cried out even more saying, "Burn her! Burn her!" And others said that if he let this woman go he would not be considered a friend of the nation or its highest authority.

19. And when the governor saw that he could not satisfy them but rather they grew infuriated, he took water and washed his hands before the religious leaders and the people and said, "I am washing my hands of this woman's blood." And they said, "Let her blood be upon us and our children."

20. And therefore he sent Drahcira to be burnt. And they stripped her and whipped her back and then led her away to be put to death. And there followed some who cried and wailed. But Drahcira, turning to them said, "Children of the earth, do not weep for me but weep for yourselves and your children. For if the way of the earth is not heeded, the day will come in which they will say, 'Blessed are the wombs which are barren and the breasts that never give milk!'"

21. And when they came to the center of the city they gave her wine to drink mingled with myrrh. And she held the cup up to the sky and said, "I now drink this blood of the earth—and this blood will comfort me. The vine which once bore the fruit from which this wine came died for me and now I shall die for the earth from whence it came."

Chapter LXI

And when they came to the stake, the executioner asked her if she had any last requests or words to say? And Drahcira asked if she could stand at the stake facing north.

2. And when they had bound her to the stake thus spoke Drahcira: "By earth—dust we are and unto dust we shall return; by air, the breath of life; by the fire of my spirit and by waters of my body—may the circle of the earth be purified. Come creatures of the earth, air, and water—come Mother Earth and Father Sky—and witness what is being done here this day. I am a letter from the earth, written not on tables of stone or parchment but upon the fleshy tables of the heart. May the smoke that ascends from my body deliver the request I ask of you O Father Sky and may the ashes of my body which fall upon the ground deliver the request I ask of you O Mother Earth—for what I have lived and taught through this body is my wish for all. So mote it be and blessed be!

3. And the governor posted a sign near the stake which all could read that said, "This is Drahcira, Prophetess of the Earth—and this was written in English, Gaelic and German."

4. But when the religious leaders saw this they said to the governor, "Don't write, 'Prophetess of the Earth' but write, 'the Witch.'" But the governor said to them, "What I have written, I have written."

5. And the executioner lit the fire. And there were those who passed by and reviled her saying, "She tried to save the earth and

she can't even save herself." And others said, "If your message is true come down from the stake and then we will believe you." And still others said, "You trusted in the way of the earth—let us see if the earth will help you now!"

6. And when the sixth hour came there was darkness over the land and Drahcira cried out with a loud voice, "I send the circle of this city into the world to do the bidding of the earth. May this be done for the good of all concerned. May life thrive now and always! In peace I came—in peace I now part. Blessed be!" And with this her head dropped to her chest and she died.

7. And her disciples saw and heard all of what became of their Teacher, and they wept bitterly.

8. Now when evening came the mother of Drahcira went to the governor and begged that she be given what remained of her daughter's bones that they might be buried. And the governor commanded that they be given to her.

9. And when she had taken them she wrapped them in a clean linen cloth and took them to the place where Drahcira and her disciples would gather.

10. And very early in the morning on the next day they divided what remained of Drahcira's bones into three piles. One pile they cast into the sea, and another they buried in the earth but the third pile they carried to that certain hill where Drahcira had communed with herself before her arrest.

11. And after they had ground this pile to powder with stones upon a great rock, they cast the powder into the air to be borne about by the wind.

Chapter LXII

And when her disciples returned to the place where they had been when Drahcira had contemplated what lay ahead for herself on the night of her arrest, they saw a piece of parchment on the ground where she had knelt. They picked it up and found that Drahcira had written upon it the following words:

2. "O Earth my Mother, my hour has come. I have glorified you as I have walked upon you and I have finished the work which you gave me to do. I have taught your ways to those who have had ears to hear.

3. "My disciples have kept your ways and they know that all things whatsoever I have given them are from you. For I have only given to them what you have given to me. And they have received these things knowing that we came from you and that you have sent us.

4. "I pray for these, for though I shall soon be no more they shall remain. Keep them, that they may be one as we are. I have taught them your ways and many will hate them as they have hated me. I ask not that they should be spared the trials that shall come upon them—for there are lessons to be learned from each but I do ask that they are able to finish their work as I have finished mine. They are set aside by your truth. And now I send them into the world as you once sent me. I do not pray only for these but for all of those who shall follow the way of the earth through their word— that they too may be one as we are. O Earth, my Mother, the world

does not truly know you but I have known you and I have declared your ways to it. May the love wherewith I have loved you be in them as well. So mote it be and blessed be!"

5. And so they went out into the world and taught all who were willing to hear the gospel of the way of the earth.

Postscript

And many other things did Drahcira teach and perform in the presence of her disciples which are not written in this book but these are written that you might believe the gospel of the way of the earth—and believing may the earth thrive now and always.

In Part II of this volume I would like to share with the reader the last message I received from Drahcira.

This message came in the literary form of a prophecy, and as with Part I which used the structure of the Gospels as its template this prophecy uses the structure of the Apocalypse, or the biblical book of Revelation as its template. Thus Drahcira's teachings can be seen in contrast with the prophetic work par excellence of the New Testament.

May the words of this prophecy move you who read to bring your life into harmony with "the way of the earth" and may you thus be included in the "remnant" described herein.

Part II

The Apocalypso:
Drahcira's Last Dance

"The Christian resolve to find the world ugly and
bad has made the world ugly and bad."
Friedrich Nietzsche

Chapter I

The revelation of the earth which came to Drahcira to show all people those things which may shortly come to pass. And she sent and signified it to her disciple, Richard who bore witness of all those things which were shown to him.

2. Blessed are they who read and they who hear the words of this prophecy and who keep those things which are written herein, for the days of the earth as we have known it may be numbered.

3. Richard, to those who dwell on the earth: Peace be to you from the earth who is our Mother and who has made us her caretakers and from Drahcira, her prophetess. Behold, if the earth departs in a cloud, woe be to the eyes that should see such a thing. And now the earth wails because of us—let us therefore comfort her.

4. I am your home and sustenance says the earth—which is and which was and which soon may not be—your Mother.

5. I Richard, who also am your brother and companion in the struggle to save the earth, was in a solitary place when I received this revelation from Drahcira. Here, while I communed with the earth, I heard a still small voice saying, "I am Drahcira, prophetess of the earth. What you see, write in a book and send it to those who dwell in the four quarters of the earth."

6. And I turned to see who spoke to me. And having turned I saw Drahcira—unclothed and standing in the midst of the four quarters of the earth. Her hair was brown as the earth, her eyes as

green as the grass and her breasts and her pelvis formed a triangle which pointed to the earth from whence we came. Her voice was as the wind which blows through the trees—as the sound of brooks of water. In her left hand she held a censer filled with burning incense and from her womb flowed the waters of life. In her right hand she held a handful of earth and from her mouth she blew out the breath of life. And her appearance was as the sun, moon and stars which shine.

7. And when I saw her I fell at her feet. Then she laid her hands upon me and said, "Fear not for it is me, Drahcira—she who once walked upon the face of the earth. Behold I am alive within you and now I hold the keys of understanding. Write the things which may be hereafter."

Chapter II

1. Unto those who live in the four quarters of the earth write, "These things say she from whose mouth is blown the breath of life:

2. "I know your works and how you have taken the gift of air and have filled it with so much uncleanness that even your children cough and choke when they breathe it—and not only this but the trees wither and die and the heavens are no longer blue but rather the color of filth.

3. "Therefore cease from the abuse of this gift or the air, which is to you the breath of life shall become the breath of death—and this judgment you will have met not only upon yourselves, but upon the whole of the earth."

4. Those who have ears let them hear what Drahcira says to all people. Those who give heed to her words shall receive the gift of air in such a way that it shall truly be unto them as the breath of life.

5. And unto those who live in the four quarters of the earth write, "These things say she who holds the censer filled with burning incense in her left hand:

6. "I know your works and how you have taken the gift of fire—of guns and bombs and napalm to scorch the earth and to torture and kill her children until the smoke of this abuse has covered the sun, moon and the stars in darkness and there has been a stench rather than the sweet smell of incense.

7. "Therefore cease from the abuse of this gift and from making weapons of fire or earth as you have known it shall be consumed and your lives will pass away with a great noise and the elements will melt with fervent heat and the earth also and the works that are therein shall be burned up."

8. Those who have ears let them hear what Drahcira says to all people. Those who give heed to her words will receive the gift of fire to use for heating and cooking and to use in such a way that it shall refresh their lives as does the sweet scent of incense.

9. And unto those who live in the four quarters of the earth write, "These things say she from whose womb flows the waters of life:

10. "I know you're your works and how you have taken the gift of water and have used it thoughtlessly—filling it with uncleanness and every abomination until it is as if the earth itself would vomit it up. Would you drink of this gift now? Well, drink it you must—and not only you but your children and your children's children. Woe be to you for this waste.

11. "Therefore cease form the abuse of this gift or the waters which you must drink to live shall become as bitter as the water of Marah and thus shall become the waters of death."

12. Those who have ears let them hear what Drahcira says to all people. Those who give heed to her words shall receive the gift of water to use for drinking, cleansing and for watering our crops. The gift of living water gives us life and sustains us.

13. And unto those who live in the four quarters of the earth write, "These things say she who holds a handful of earth in her right hand:

14. "I know your works and how you have taken the gift of the earth and have filled it with things which are hard for her to digest—things which though they may seem sweet to you but which are bitter in the belly of the earth. And while the earth would not have these things, you continue to stuff it full of every abominable thing. And thus you are making the earth into a dung heap.

15. "Therefore cease from the abuse of this gift or the earth, which you have worked in the sweat of your brow, shall no longer yield you its fruit in due season but shall rather become as a place of refuse."

16. Those who have ears let them hear what Drahcira says to all people. Those who give heed to her words shall receive the gift of the earth in such a way that the earth shall give of its plenty and it shall be to you as the Garden of Eden.

Chapter III

After this I looked and behold—a door was opened in my mind and the first voice which I heard was as the wind which blows through the trees—as the sound of water brooks. And it said, "Come with me and I will show you the things which may soon be."

2. And immediately I was in the spirit and I saw a circle was cast and one stood in the middle of it.

3. And she who stood there was very beautiful to look upon.

4. And round her were twelve others clothed with the sky. Four of these stood in the directions of the four winds.

5. The first stood at the east of the circle and held a cage with four doves. Her hair was white.

6. The second stood at the south of the circle and held a censer filled with incense. His hair was red.

7. The third stood at the west of the circle and held a vessel filled with water. Her hair was black.

8. The fourth stood at the north of the circle and held a handful of earth. His hair was brown.

9. And then as I beheld, I heard these four say, "Holy, holy, holy, O Earth our Mother, which is and which was and which soon may not be."

10. And whenever these four give glory and honor and thanks to the earth, the others in the circle fall down saying, "You are

worthy O Earth to receive glory, honor and thanks for you are our home and sustenance and have given us many things for our pleasure—for truly, 'all acts of love and pleasure are your rituals.'"[1]

---

1   This line is from "The Charge of the Goddess" by Doreen Valiente.

Chapter IV

And I saw in the left hand of her who stood in the middle of the circle a book which was sealed with four seals.

2. And then I heard one proclaiming with a loud voice, "Who is able to open the book and to loose its seals?"

3. And though many were able to open the book none would.

4. And I wept much because no one was found who would open the book and read what was in it.

5. But then one of those who stood in the circle said to me, "Weep not, for behold the prophetess of the earth has prevailed to open the book and to loose its seals."

6. And I beheld and in the middle of the circle lay Drahcira in the form of a star—with arms and legs outstretched. And the book was on her stomach as if her body was a living altar.

7. And those who stood in the direction of the four winds sang a new song saying,

> "The prophetess
> Shall open the book
> And loose the seals thereof.
> And those who will
> Must stop and read
> Its message given in love.

"A warning shall
Each seal reveal
That we might change our ways.
To save the earth
We all must move
To heal the Ancient of Days."

8. And then I heard the voices of all of those in the circle chanting these words until the sound of their voices rose in power and then reached into the heart of every person on the earth who was willing to receive them.

9. And though these did not know what it was that had reached into their hearts, they did sense that a message had come to them in love to show them what may shortly come to pass.

Chapter V

And I saw when Drahcira opened the first seal, and I heard as it were the noise of thunder. And her who stood at the east of the circle said, "Come and see."

2. And I looked and saw a white horse which carried cages filled with doves. And she who stood at the east of the circle opened the cages and all but one flew away. Therefore she reached into the cage and took the dove in her hands, and casting it up into the sky she said, "We call upon you to be our witness O Father Sky. How can we ever thank you enough, for you have breathed into our nostrils the breath of life and thus we live." Having said this, she knelt down and kissed Drahcira on her left hand. But then I looked and lo, the air became as the smoke of a furnace and the fowls that flew in the midst of the heavens fell to the earth even as a fig tree casts its untimely figs when it is shaken by a mighty wind. And then I heard the voices of all of those in the circle say,

> "A warning has
> Each seal revealed,
> Thus we must change our ways.

> "To save the earth
> We all must move
> To heal the Ancient of Days."

3. And when she had opened the second seal, I heard him who stood at the south of the circle say, "Come and see."

4. And I looked and saw a red horse which carried in its saddle bags incense. And he who stood at the south of the circle took some of the incense and put it into his censer and then waving it unto the rising sun he said, "We call on you to be our witness O sun, moon and stars that we thank you for shining your light upon us." And having said this, he knelt down and kissed Drahcira's feet. But then I looked and lo, the forests of the earth were on fire and the sun became black as sackcloth and the moon became as blood and the stars of the heavens were obscured from my sight. And then I heard the voices of all of those in the circle say,

> "A warning has
> Each seal revealed,
> Thus we must change our ways.
>
> "To save the earth
> We all must move
> To heal the Ancient of Days."

5. And when she had opened the third seal, I heard her who stood to the west of the circle say, "Come and see."

6. And there was another horse that was black which carried buckets of water wherein a few fishes were. And she who stood at the west of the circle cupped her hands and drew water from the buckets and poured it upon the earth near Drahcira's right hand saying, "We call on you waters of the earth and all that live therein to be our witnesses." We are thankful for the waters that cleanse, refresh and give life." And having said this, she knelt down and kissed Drahcira on her right hand. But then I looked and lo, the sea and rivers and the fountains of water became as bitter as the water of Marah and many of the creatures which were in the water died. And then I heard the voices of all of those in the circle say,

"A warning has
Each seal revealed,
Thus we must change our ways.

"To save the earth
We all must move
To heal the Ancient of Days."

7. And when she had opened the fourth seal, I heard him who stood at the north of the circle say, "Come and see."

8. And I looked and saw a brown horse which carried saddle bags with some dirt. And he who stood at the north of the circle took a handful of dirt from the saddle bag and sprinkled it upon the earth saying, "We call upon you to be our witness O Mother Earth. How can we ever thank you enough, for we are bone of your bone and flesh of your flesh, in that we are dust. And this dirt which is of the earth sustains us with its bounty of crops, vineyards, and beautiful flowers and trees which delight our eyes. You are here for all without price." And having said this he knelt down and kissed Drahcira on the forehead. But then I looked and lo, the fruitful place was as a desert and the whole land was desolate and those who remained mourned and groaned in pain together. And then I heard the voices of all of those in the circle say,

"A warning has
Each seal revealed,
Thus we must change our ways.

"To save the earth
We all must move
To heal the Ancient of Days."

Chapter VI

And after these things I saw those who stood in the directions of the four winds and they bound the circle that it should not be undone until the appointed time.

2. And I saw her who lay in the middle of the circle rise up and she held within her hands a light which glowed as a star which shows itself as a jewel in the night. And she cried out with a loud voice to those who stood in the directions of the four winds, "Loose not the circle until all those who are willing to see, behold the light which glows within them!"

3. And I heard the number of those in whom the light glowed and it was billions. And after this I beheld and lo, I saw billions of people of all nations, kindred and tongues and they all glowed with the light from within—and yet many could not see the light which glows within.

4. And I cried out with a loud voice saying, "The salvation which all have sought in heaven is within all and is a part of we who are of the earth!"

5. And all those who stood in the circle said, "The light glows within all and all glow with the light!"

6. And I asked Drahcira, "Why do so many not see the light which glows within?"

7. And she said to me, "It is because the cares of life and the deceitfulness of riches so fill their sight that they are blind to their true nature and thus having eyes they do not see. But in truth, if all would see who they are, all would live in peace and none would hunger anymore, neither would they thirst."

Chapter VII

And again I saw those who stood in the directions of the four winds and to them were given four flutes.

2. And she who had lain as a living altar took much incense that she might offer it up with the requests of those who stood in the circle. And the smoke of the incense ascended up unto Father Sky. And there were voices and thunderings and lightnings.

3. And when she who stood at the east of the circle sounded her flute, I saw doves flying in the midst of the heavens, and the heavens were filled with all forms of winged life. And the doves which I saw flew with grace and I felt gratitude for all of this.

4. And when he who stood at the south of the circle sounded his flute, I saw salamanders walking through fire which cleanses and prepares the way for rebirth and renewal as in the legend of the Phoenix. And the salamanders which I saw walked with grace and I felt gratitude for this.

5. And when she who stood at the west of the circle sounded her flute, I saw schools of fishes swimming in the sea and all of the waters of the earth teamed with life. And the fish which I saw swam with grace and I felt gratitude for of all of this.

6. And when he who stood at the north of the circle sounded his flute, I saw dogs running upon the earth and the whole of the earth was filled with more species then could be counted. And the dogs which I saw ran with grace and I felt gratitude for all of this.

7. And those who stood in the directions of the four winds piped their pipes and all nature sang their praises unto the earth saying, "You are worthy O Earth to receive glory, honor and thanks for you are our home and sustenance and have given us many things for our pleasure."

Chapter VIII

And then I saw Drahcira, clothed with a cloud, and a rainbow encircled her head, and her face was as the sun, and with her feet she stood firmly upon the earth.

2. And she held in her hands a cake which was sweeter than honey, and she cried out with a loud voice—and her voice was as the wind which blows through the trees—as the sound of water brooks.

3. And when she cried out, the four winds blew. And when the four winds had uttered their voices, I was about to write when I heard Drahcira say to me, "Seal up those things which the four winds uttered and write them not for those who dwell upon the earth are not ready to hear what the four winds would say to them."

4. Then she who stood firmly upon the earth turned to the east and swore by the breath of life, and to the south she swore by the fire of her spirit, and to the west she swore by the waters of her body and to the north she swore by her own flesh—that there must be no more delay!

5. For when she who stood at the east of the circle sounded her flute and doves flew in the midst of the heavens with grace she saw that without peace, whose symbol is the dove, there shall be time for us no longer.

6. Then he who stood at the north of the circle spoke to me and said, "Go take the cake from the hands of she who stands firmly upon the earth."

7. And I went up to her and said to her, "Give me the cake that I might eat it." And she said to me, "Take it and eat it up and it shall be sweeter than honey in your mouth but it shall be bitter in your belly."

8. And so I took the cake from Drahcira's hands and ate it up and it was in my mouth sweeter than honey but as soon as I had eaten it my belly was bitter.

9. And she said to me, "As this cake was sweet in your mouth and yet bitter in your belly, so are the works of our race upon the earth. Let all think on these things…"

Chapter IX

And there was given me a great cord, and Drahcira said, "Rise and cast a circle as far as the cord will reach that you may measure the circumference of the most holy place."

2. And when I cast it I found that the cord encircled the whole of the earth and that nothing was left out.

3. And then Drahcira said to me, "Within the circle of the earth there are seven who shall show forth the mysteries of life clothed only with the sky.

4. "These seven are: male and female, female and female, male and male and bisexuals—each after their kind and their witness is as the sun showing forth its light at noonday.

5. "And if any would try to silence their witness, creation itself would immediately cry out, 'Though all are not the same we must nurture the diversity that is upon the earth!'

6. "These seven are witnesses and symbols of the diversity of life on earth. They are filled with the breath of life, the fire of the spirit, the water of life and they as all of us shall return to dust, for dust we are and unto dust shall we return."

7. But when they labored to show forth the mysteries of life, the Corporations which are the enemy of life and spirit made war against them that it might overcome them and kill them.

8. But as they lay together, moved by the fire of their spirits, a remnant of all nations, kindred, tongues and peoples rejoiced because of them and because these seven did not fear to show

forth the mysteries of life. And in their boldness they overcame the Corporations!

9. And after nine months, life came forth from the womb of one of the women and great joy fell upon the other women and the men as well.

10. And I heard a great voice saying to all who had ears to hear, "This is but one of my beloved children, in whom I am well pleased—but so are all of those who live within the circle of the earth, for truly this is the most holy place and therefore all are holy who dwell herein."

11. And then as I listened I heard the voices of all those who stood in the circle say, "We give thanks, O Earth our mother—which is, and which was, but which soon may not be, for you are filled with life and that abundantly. Therefore we shall honor you by honoring all life."

12. And then my eyes were opened and I saw the earth "As It Is," and in truth it is the most holy place—as Drahcira once taught, "The earth itself is a temple—a temple which we have defiled."

Chapter X

And there appeared a great wonder in the heavens—Earth clothed with the sun—and the moon at her feet and upon her head a crown made up of the stars of the heavens.

2. And she was with child and longed to be delivered.

3. And there appeared another wonder—Corporations which walked upon two legs—dreadful, terrible and exceedingly strong. And with great teeth they devoured and broke things into pieces and then stamped out what remained with their feet. And they had mouths speaking great things.

4. And the Corporations stood upon the Earth which was ready to give birth—for they wanted to devour her children as soon as they were born.

5. And Earth brought forth herbs and trees bearing their fruits and creatures of the land and sea and air and I saw that it was good.

6. But when the Corporations saw her children, they began to devour them and many did not endure—neither was there place for them any more upon the earth.

7. And I heard a loud voice saying, "Woe unto the children of the earth for the Corporations have come upon you having great greed and they knows not that they have but a short time."

8. But Earth did not have wings like an eagle that she might fly away from the Corporations and so she waited for someone to deliver her. And her deliverer was the remnant of every nation, kindred, tongue and people who were opposed to the Corporations.

9. And as I watched them protest and resist I saw that the head of the Corporations was wounded unto death—but then the deadly wound was healed and the world was amazed at the Head of the Corporations.

10. And they worshiped the Corporations saying, "What is comparable to the Corporations? Who is able to stop them?"

11. And the Corporations' mouth spoke great things and they made war with the remnant, and though the world worshiped the Corporations, the remnant would not.

12. If any have ears, let them hear: "Those who lead into captivity shall go into captivity and those who kill with the sword shall be killed with the sword. As the law has said, 'Whatsoever we sow, that shall we also reap.'"

13. And the Corporations did great wonders, even making fire come down from the heavens upon the earth with their weapons for all to see.

14. And the Corporations deceived the people by means of these wonders which they had the power to do. And with their great mouths the Corporations said that whosoever would not buy from them should die.

15. And they caused all, both small and great, rich and poor, free and bond to accept their workings either in thought or in cooperative actions and that no one might buy or sell unless they conformed in these ways.

16. Here is wisdom. Let those with understanding see the Corporations for what they truly are—self-centered centers of greed which have no concern for the earth or the people so long as they continue to make money, for their God is Mammon. And they have many numbers and many names.

Chapter XI

And I looked, and lo, Drahcira stood on a mountain and with her the remnant of every nation, kindred, tongue and people who could see the light which did shine forth from all—however dim it might be.

2. And I heard a voice, as the voice of many waters, and as the voice of a great thunder, and I heard the voice of singers singing.

3. And they sang a new song before Drahcira and all of those in the circle, but those who worshiped the Corporations did not sing this song.

4. Those who sing are they who follow the way of the earth.

5. And I saw Drahcira standing upon the mountain having the gospel of the way of the earth to teach all those who dwell upon the earth saying with a loud voice, "Fear not the Corporations, nor give them glory, for the hour of their judgment will come. Rather give glory to the sun, moon and stars, and to the waters, earth and sky.

6. "For the kingdom of the Corporations shall fall—because it has made all nations drink the blood of the earth.

7. "And know this, that whosoever shall worship the Corporations and conform to their image shall have their blood poured out without mixture into the cup of greed. And they shall be tormented knowing that they had helped the Corporations spill the innocent blood of the earth.

8. "Here however lies the patience of the remnant: It lies in knowing that they have defended the defenseless and have spoken on behalf of that which could not speak."

9. And when I looked up, behold a white cloud which carried rain with which to nourish the earth. And when I looked down from the mountain I saw that the fields were ripe for the harvest.

10. And as the harvest moon shown down upon the whitened fields and as Drahcira stood upon the mountain I heard a still small voice—the voice of the earth—say, "though they slay me, yet will I serve them."

Chapter XII

And as the moon shone full in the midst of the heavens I saw those who stood in the circle. And they did chant the words of Drahcira,

> 2. "Oh Earth, our home—
> Holy be your name.
> Your kingdom yet endures—
> Thus let your will be done
> As it was in days past.
> Give us this day our daily bread
> And forgive us where we have failed you
> Even as we forgive those who have failed us.
> And let us not be led to betray you
> But deliver us from such temptations.
> For you are our home and our sustenance—
> May we thus honor you forever.
> Blessed be!"

3. And after that I looked, and behold Drahcira stood in the middle of the circle and held a golden vase in her hands full of water drawn from a crystal well. And when the moon shown bright in the water of the vase she handed the vase to him who stood in the south of the circle saying, "Pour out this vase upon the earth, and may the plague that the Corporations bring be thus diluted."

4. And when I looked, lo a plague spread upon the earth which was toxic and grievous.

5. And I heard her who stood in the west of the circle say, "The Corporations are to the earth what cancer is to the body."

6. And I saw that the Corporations had covered the earth with blood and that their filth was heaped from the depths of the sea unto the heavens. And though their kingdom filled the whole world with darkness, those who worshiped the Corporations blasphemed the earth for their suffering and did not repent of their deeds.

Chapter XIII

And there came she who poured the vase upon the earth and she talked with me saying to me, "Come here and I will show you the judgment of the great Corporations."

2. So she carried me away into a great city and I saw the great Corporations, and they walked on two legs, dreadful and terrible—arrayed in purple and scarlet, and decked with gold and precious stones and having gold chalices in their hands full of the blood of the earth.

3. And upon their foreheads were no name and all names.

4. And I saw that the Corporations were drunk with the blood of the earth, and when I saw it I was amazed.

5. And she who poured out the vase said to me, "Why are you amazed? I will tell you the mystery of the Corporations which walk on two legs.

6. "The Corporations that you saw are, but were not always as you have seen them. They ascended out of the bottomless pit and shall there one day return.

7. "And the Corporations have one mind, and those who worship them give it its strength and power."

8. And after these things I heard Earth cry out with a strong voice saying, "Come out of them my children, that you be not partakers of their plagues. For they shall reap what they have sown, and the cup that they have filled with my blood shall be filled unto it double.

9. "Therefore their judgment shall surely come. And they shall be utterly destroyed.

10. "And when that time comes, the kings of the earth who have lived in luxury with them shall bewail them and lament for them saying, 'Alas, alas that great power, that mighty power, who gave us authority over the earth has fallen!'

11. "And the merchants of the world shall weep and mourn over them, for there shall be none to buy their merchandise any more—

12. "the merchandise of gold, silver, jewels and oil—all things which were for the rich shall depart.

13. "And the merchants of these and many other things which were made rich by the Corporations shall stand afar off for fear of their judgment—weeping and wailing and saying, 'Alas, alas that great power, that mighty power that once cause us to be arrayed in purple and scarlet and decked with gold and precious stones has fallen!'

14. "And all those who traded by sea, land and air cried when they saw that the Corporations had fallen. And they cast dust on their heads and cried, weeping and wailing saying, 'Alas, alas, that great power, that mighty power wherein we were made rich is now desolate!'"

15. And though I saw that the Corporations had fallen as a great millstone cast into the depths of the sea, I could not rejoice because of the plagues they had brought upon the earth.

16. And when I had seen these things I knew that the question was not, "Would the Corporations fall?"—for surely they will, but rather "Would the earth live on after this fall?" And Drahcira assured me that it would...

Chapter XIV

And I saw what should become of the earth if judgment did not fall upon the Corporations swiftly.

2. And I beheld and lo, it was without form and void. And there were no humans and the birds of the heavens were no more.

3. And the fruitful places were wildernesses and all the cities were broken down and the whole land was desolate.

4. But then I saw the earth as it once was in its virgin beauty—apart from what the Corporations had done.

5. And I saw a pure river of water, clear as crystal, and trees bearing all manner of fruit. I saw grass and herb yielding seeds after their kinds. And there were mountains covered with snow, valleys filled with every beast of the field and deserts wrapped in their silent solitude. I saw the great oceans teaming with life and every manner of bird which flew in the heavens. And there was night and day, winter and spring, death and life—and all was good. For all moved with grace as the wheel of the years turned.

6. And after these things I heard Drahcira speak saying, "You are worthy O Earth to receive glory, honor and thanks for you are our home and sustenance and have given us many things for our pleasure."

7. And she said to me, "Blessed is the remnant of every nation, kindred, tongue and people for they have lived true unto the earth our mother."

8. And I fell at her feet to worship her and she said to me, "Do not do this for I am only your fellow servant and of the remnant who have walked in the way of the earth. Serve the earth and she shall serve you well."

9. I Richard saw these things and heard them. And when I had heard and seen them, I wrote them down that you might know those things which might shortly come to pass.

10. And Drahcira said to me, "Seal not the sayings of this prophecy for the time is at hand.

11. "I Drahcira have led you to testify to these things that those who dwell upon the earth might be forewarned. May the earth thrive now and always. Blessed be!"

Printed in the United States
By Bookmasters